An Introduc
West African Animal Ecology

A reservoir showing depth gauge

Frontispiece

An Introduction to
West African Animal Ecology

C. I. O. Olaniyan, B.Sc., Ph.D.
Professor of Zoology
School of Biological Sciences
University of Lagos

HEINEMANN EDUCATIONAL BOOKS LTD
LONDON AND IBADAN

Heinemann Educational Books Ltd
LONDON EDINBURGH MELBOURNE
AUCKLAND TORONTO HONG KONG
SINGAPORE KUALA LUMPUR IBADAN
NAIROBI LUSAKA NEW DELHI

ISBN 0 435 93673 5

© C. I. O. Olaniyan 1968, 1975
First Published 1968
Second Edition 1975

Published by Heinemann Educational Books Ltd
48 Charles Street, London W1X 8AH

PMB 5205 Ibadan

Printed in Great Britain by
Butler & Tanner Ltd, Frome and London

Contents

Part I Environment

1 What is ecology? — 3
2 Habitat and environment — 7
3 Ecological factors — 16
4 The adaptation of animals — 37

Part II Animal species ecology

5 Marine and lagoon animals—I — 55
6 Marine and lagoon animals—II — 80
7 Freshwater animals — 101
8 Land animals — 116

Part III Population and community ecology

9 The interrelationships of animals — 151
Select Bibliography — 164
Index — 165

List of Plates

Frontispiece
A reservoir showing depth gauge[6]

Facing page 58
I Life on rhizophore of *Rhizophora racemosa*[6]

Facing page 59
II *Kingfisher*, Lagos[1]

Between pages 92 and 93
III Throwing a cast net on Lagos lagoon[6]
IV Breeding behaviour of *Tilapia heudeloti*[2]
V Breeding behaviour of *Tilapia heudeloti*[2] (cont'd)
VI Giant termitarium of *Macrotermes* near Jebba[6]

Facing page 124
VII Some minute soil animals[5]

Facing page 125
VIII Common millipedes of forest soil[4]

Facing page 144
IX Dog-faced baboon, *Papio anubis*[6]

Facing page 145
X Rock Fauna[5]

Acknowledgements for Plates

1 Federal Fisheries Service, Lagos.
2 Dr Lester Aronson, New York.
3 Russel: World of the Soil (Collins).
4 Dr Afolabi Toye, Ibadan.
5 Mr R. B. Walker, Zaria.
6 The author.

Preface

The study of ecology is at present so much neglected at school and college level in West Africa, that most students only recognize it as one of the many 'ologies' of modern times. Because these 'ologies' turn up more frequently in the biological sciences than in the physical sciences, they have a vague hint that it is a biological subject. A common reaction to this ignorance on the part of students is to blame the school teachers, but the school teachers point out that there is no single local text book on the subject except for A. J. Carpenter's *West African Nature Study* which was written in the thirties, and has an elementary school approach. They explain further that it would be ridiculous to use text books intended for countries in temperate climates in a subject such as ecology, where the emphasis should be on local problems.

I think that the teachers are right, and one reason for writing this book is to meet their challenge. During the past fifteen years or so, beginning with the opening of biology departments in the universities of West Africa, a few biologists have done some useful pioneer work in ecology, and their results and mine form the basis for this book.

The second, and perhaps more important reason for this book is a desire to stimulate the study of biology in the field especially among young people, whether they intend to specialize in biology or not. Nowadays, the picture of the typical biologist seems to be of a person in a white coat dissecting an animal in the laboratory, and no longer that of a 'naturalist' who spends his time studying in the field. In Europe, up till the end of the nineteenth century, the typical biologist was the naturalist. Thousands of people, including those without formal scientific training, spent much of their time in the study of natural history and much of the biological knowledge of today was derived from their study. Natural history is no longer fashionable in Europe. The new biological subjects such as genetics, cellular physiology, and biochemistry are on the ascendant; and they attract more and more students. It is perhaps possible to be a biologist today without ever seeing a whole plant or whole animal! But should this trend be followed in West Africa or the other developing countries of the world? I do not think so, because the knowledge of our plants and animals today is probably at the level that obtained in Europe in the eighteenth century, and in view of this we cannot afford to neglect ecology which is an essential base on which the more sophisticated biological studies can be built.

This book is not based on any particular examination syllabus, but would be suitable for teachers, and students in the sixth form, or in their first year at university. It is also intended to be easily understood and enjoyed by people without formal training in biology. Such people are, in fact, indispensable in the building up of a community of naturalists so essential for the growth of biological knowledge in our part of the world.

If after reading this book, any one is encouraged to study animals or plants in the field, then my hopes will have been fulfilled.

Note to Second Edition

I am delighted to have an early opportunity to revise this publication for two reasons. Firstly, it has given me a chance to correct a number of obvious errors both in the text and the drawings, and secondly, I have had an opportunity to add some useful up-to-date information. A general bibliography, primarily for the teacher, is added at the end of the book. However, the general plan remains the same and no major changes have been made.

I wish to thank those colleagues who have pointed out mistakes in the text and drawings. I also acknowledge with thanks the use of drawings from G. S. Cansdale's *West African Snakes*, J. H. Elgood's *Birds of the West African Town and Garden* and Booth's *Small Mammals of West Africa*. Finally, I wish to thank the Dean of the University of Miami, School of Marine Science, Dr F. G. Walton Smith, and the Chairman of the Division of Biology, Dr Gilbert L. Voss, for granting me facilities at their institution where most of the work on the preparation of the second edition was carried out during a sabbatical leave from the University of Lagos.

Acknowledgements

I would like to express my thanks to all who have assisted me in the preparation of this book. First to my wife Mrs B. F. Olaniyan, and my former teacher and colleague at the University of Ibadan, Prof. J. H. Elgood, for their encouragement and assistance without which the book would not have been produced at all. I might warn that it takes a lot of encouragement to get a university teacher to decide on spending time and energy in producing a pre-university text book instead of writing papers for scientific journals!

My thanks also go to my secretarial staff who have typed the manuscripts, to Mr Frank Price for his drawings, and to Messrs Heinemann Educational Books Ltd for being such helpful publishers to work with.

Plates and drawings from various sources are gratefully acknowledged elsewhere in this book.

C. I. O. O.

Lagos, Nigeria,
January, 1968.

Part 1: Environment

1: What is ecology?

When a chapter in a book is headed with a question, a definition is usually expected to follow. I do not like definitions, but I know that most students do. I do not like them because there is always a temptation to memorize them without necessarily having a proper understanding of the subject; and I suppose many students like them for precisely that reason! It should be well understood that the reason for giving a definition is to present an idea in a nutshell, which is a good thing in itself. It is more important, however, to understand the idea that is being presented so well, that you are able to give your own definition rather than repeating the orthodox one mechanically.

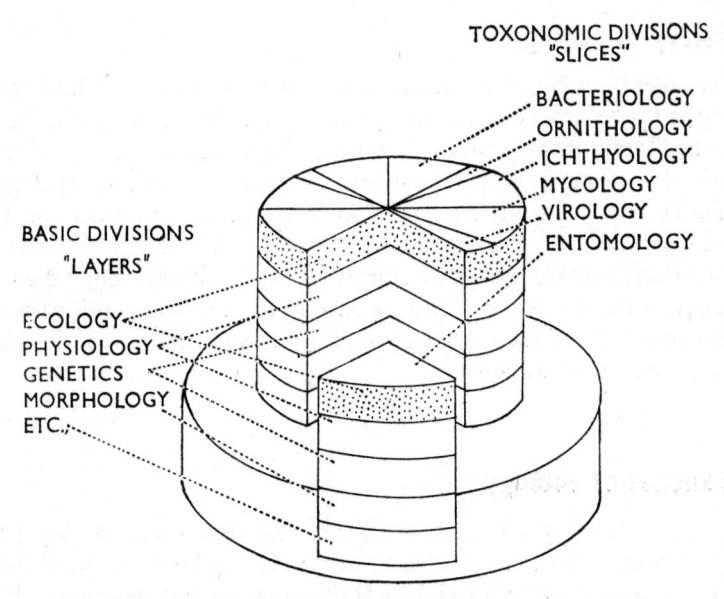

Fig. 1. The 'biological cake' (after Odum).

Ecology is defined as **the study of living organisms in relation to their environment.** The word 'ecology' is derived from the Greek word *Oikos* meaning 'house'. In other words ecology can also be described as the study of living organisms at home. It is therefore essentially a field science unlike some other branches of biology such as anatomy and physiology which usually involve the transfer of the organisms to the laboratory, either to dissect or to perform experiments with them.

Ecology is a *basic* biological science because it deals with *all living organisms.* Its scope is therefore very extensive. We can speak of plant ecology, insect ecology, the ecology of parasites, and so on. Even the study of human populations falls within the field of ecology. To use an analogy of Odum (see Fig. 1), ecology is a layer in the *biological cake,* and whenever a slice is cut, some ecology is cut with it!

Apart from being a layer of the biological cake, ecology is also a small part of the *physico-chemical cake.* It is therefore not a purely biological subject. This is because its study involves *the environment as well as the organism,* and in studying the environment, its physical and chemical characteristics are quite relevant.

History of ecology

Like other branches of the sciences, ecology must have had a history as long as that of man himself. Early man, in order to survive, must have 'studied' some ecology although he obviously would not have given the study that name. Perhaps it was just a branch of 'food findingology', since he required a good knowledge of the other organisms and his environment to do this efficiently. It was in 1869 that the biologist *Ernst Haeckel (1834–1919)* first coined the word 'ecology'; but it did not become a recognized branch of science in its own right until early in this century. Since then it has grown considerably and is now divisible into a number of sections.

Branches of ecology

Ecology is broadly divided into *plant ecology* and *animal ecology* and it is with the latter that we shall be dealing in this book. These distinctions, of course, like most biological divisions, are not water-tight. For example, one finds that a study of types of vegetation is essential for understanding the ecology of land animals. In many aspects, plant and animal ecology are inseparable; and a more appropriate approach to ecological study is to treat it under four aspects, namely, (*a*) *species ecology,* (*b*) *population ecology,* (*c*) *community ecology,* and (*d*) *ecosystem ecology,* without a division into plant and animal ecology. These are simply different aspects of the subject, and there is no doubt that with further study more sub-divisions will appear. In fact, this is regarded as a better approach to the subject. In effect, what is covered here is mainly animal species ecology as the bulk of Part II, preceded by a study of environment in Part I, and with a final chapter on elementary aspects of population and community ecology in Part III.

Relationship with genetics

Ecology cannot be treated in isolation, since, as previously stated, it is related to other branches of biology and even to the physical sciences; its very close relationship with genetics deserves special mention. Ecology and genetics are about the same age, although this does not explain their close relationship which arises from the fact that genetics deals with **heredity** and **environment** and ecology deals with **organism** and **environment,** so that, in the study of environment, we have a field in which they clearly overlap.

Things to do

(i) Find out what you can about Ernst Haeckel (1834–1919). Look him up in the section on history of science in your library. You will find that apart from coining the word 'ecology' he contributed to biological knowledge in other fields.

(ii) Find out from people in your home area what they know of any effects of climate, soil, plants, etc. on any animals of interest to you in the area; attempt to verify some of this information by your own observations.

(iii) List the various branches of biological science and differentiate between the slices and layers of the 'biological cake'.

2: Habitat and environment

Definitions

'Habitat' and 'environment' are two words commonly used in every-day speech to indicate the location of living organisms. The habitat of an animal, you often hear people say, is where it 'lives'; and its environment is its 'surroundings'.

The word *habitat*, in ecological study, does not denote a particular place, rather it **denotes areas which sustain life, and which have similar physical or chemical constituents.** In other words, habitat is used here as a collective noun. Hence, when we speak of the marine habitat, we mean any body of water with the physical and chemical constitution of sea water. In this way we can identify three main habitats, (*a*) marine habitat, (*b*) freshwater habitat, and (*c*) terrestrial habitat.

Each of these habitats in ecological language is a *biota,* and the word *biosphere* is used to describe all these habitats collectively, as **comprising all the available habitable areas of the Earth,** be it sea, freshwater or land.

In everyday speech, 'environment' means 'surroundings', but in ecology the environment of an organism is described more precisely, firstly in terms of **the physical nature of its habitat, called its 'abiotic environment',** and secondly in terms of **all other living organisms associated with it in that habitat, which constitute its 'biotic environment'.** In short, **the environment is the sum total of all the external factors affecting an organism.** If we consider a fish in a lake therefore, its habitat is freshwater, its abiotic environment consists of the physical and chemical features of freshwater, and its biotic environment consists of the plants and animals in the lake. Given an even wider meaning, environment includes the *'internal environment'* of the organism, consisting primarily of its body fluids. When considering the 'surroundings' of an organism, therefore, we have to bear in mind its abiotic, biotic, and internal environments.

It may be noted that in the study of internal environment, we have a sphere in which ecology overlaps with physiology.

Ecological zones

Each major habitat is divided into a number of ecological zones.

(a) Marine habitat

Figure 2 shows the various zones of the marine habitat.

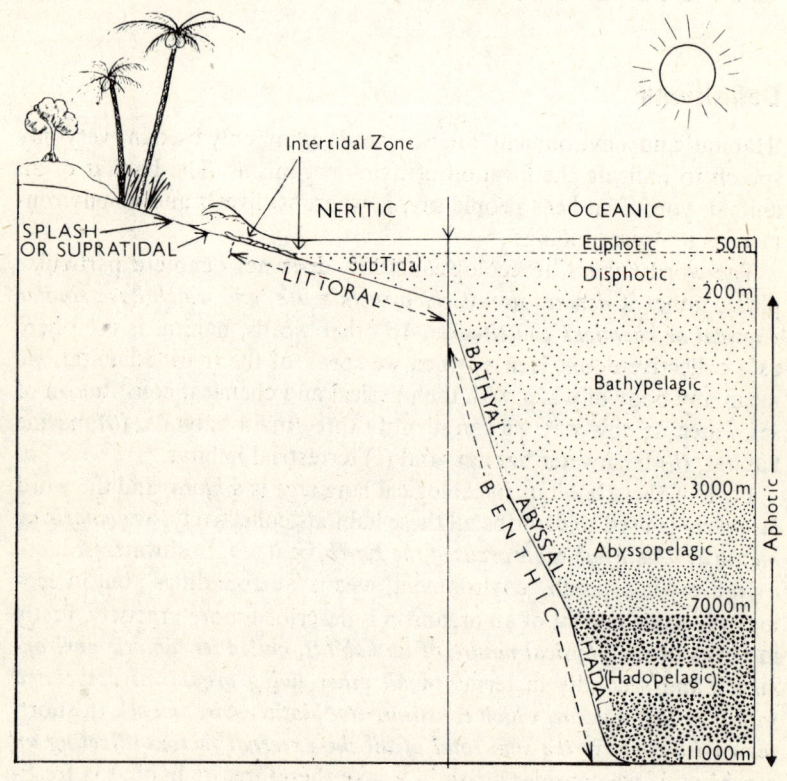

Fig. 2. Zones of the marine habitat.

A systematic way of dealing with this figure is to consider first the zones along the bottom or substratum, which are as follows:

(i) *Supratidal zone or splash zone:* Although this is technically not an aquatic zone, since it is never submerged by water, it can be included here as where the marine and land habitats meet. The waves splash over it, especially when there is a rocky shore, and continuously spray it with sea water.

HABITAT AND ENVIRONMENT

(ii) *Intertidal zone:* Area submerged by water at high tide but exposed at low tide. (Tides are explained in Chapter 3.)
(iii) *Subtidal zone:* Bottom, lying along the continental shelf, varying in depth considerably from a few to 200 metres, but never exposed.
(iv) *Bathyal zone:* Bottoms ranging between 200 metres and 3000 metres deep.
(v) *Abyssal zone:* Bottoms ranging between 3000 metres, and 7000 metres deep.
(vi) *Hadal zone:* Bottoms more than 7000 metres deep.

The limits of the last three zones are somewhat variable and you may find in other books that the depths given are different. One may reasonably substitute the words 'deep', 'very deep', and 'very, very deep'. The hadal zone (derived from the word Hades) will no doubt be of some interest, because you will now realize that there is an alternative to the biblical 'hell fire'!

It is important to understand Fig. 2 properly. You may get a mistaken idea if the figure is not viewed three-dimensionally. The drop from the edge of the continental shelf to 10 000 metres *is representative of all the oceans of the world.* The depth of the ocean floor varies a great deal, because as we have hills, valleys, and mountains on land, so we have them under the sea. A very high undersea mountain or plateau breaks the surface to form an island, and a very deep valley forms a trench. The deepest point so far recorded is *the Mariana trench in the Philippines* with a depth of 11 500 metres (6 miles). If you were to drop the Himalayas into this trench, they would be completely covered. There may be deeper trenches which are still undiscovered. In spite of the great variability in the depths of the sea, a mean of about 4 000 metres has been estimated for all the oceans, compared with the mean height of land above sea level estimated as 850 metres.

Next, let us get away from the bottom and consider the zones within the water itself. The waters over the continental shelf are described as *neritic*, meaning near to land; and those beyond the edge of the shelf over the deep waters as *oceanic.* Within these waters three zones are distinguished.

(i) *Euphotic zone* which includes the surface waters down to any depths to which enough light can penetrate to make photosynthesis possible. The depth to which light penetrates varies considerably but 50 metres is average for the euphonic zone.
(ii) *Disphotic zone* to which light penetrates, but not enough for photosynthesis. The limit of the disphotic zone is about 200 metres.

(iii) *Aphotic zone:* the waters of total darkness. This is divisible into bathypelagic, abyssopelagic and hadopelagic zones.

Before considering the freshwater habitat, it would be useful to point out that the areas where marine and freshwater meet present such interesting conditions and problems that they are sometimes constituted into a separate habitat—namely the **brackish water habitat**. Bodies of water such as coastal lagoons and estuaries fall into this category.

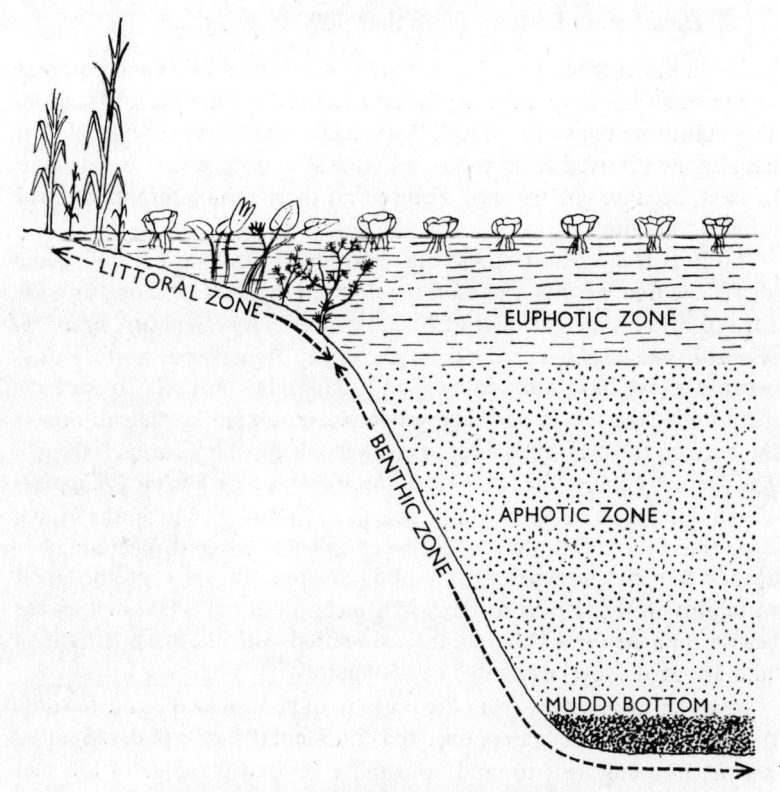

Fig. 3. Zones of the lentic freshwater habitat.

(b) *Freshwater habitat*

The freshwater habitat consists of two types: lakes, ponds, and other standing water described as **lentic** (from *lentis*, meaning 'calm') and running water such as rivers and streams described as **lotic** (from *lotus* meaning 'washed'). To avoid confusing these two words, it is useful to remember that in one Nigerian language (Yoruba) the first two

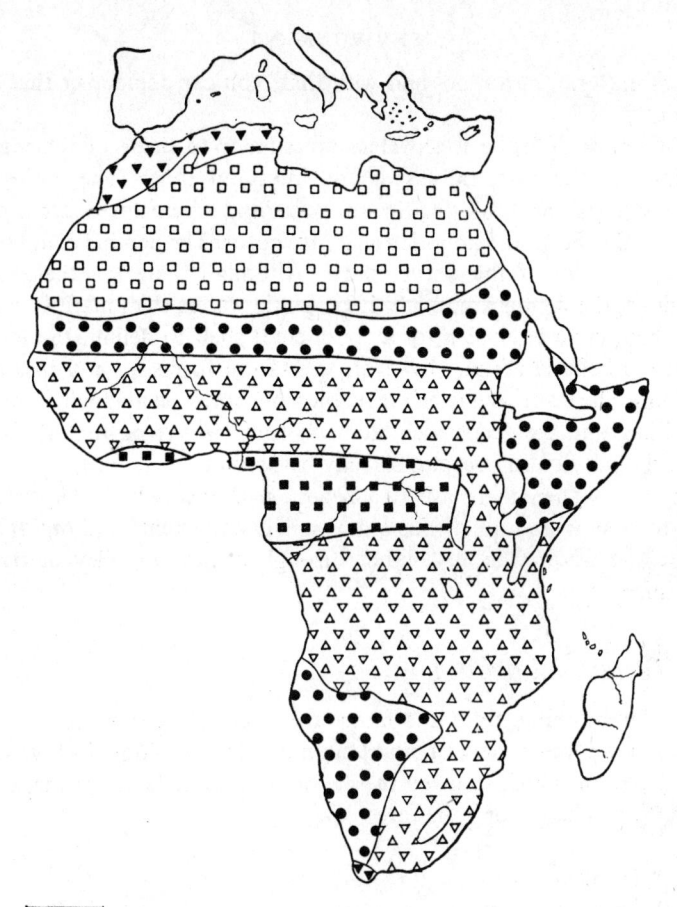

Fig. 4. Map of Africa showing land zones (after Odum).

letters in 'lotic' mean 'go' and with that, you can remember that lotic waters 'go'!

The zones of lentic freshwaters are similar to those of the marine except that there are no supra- and intertidal zones. The bottom of shallow parts constitute the littoral zone, and where the water is deep enough, disphotic and aphotic zones also occur. The benthic zone covers the substratum of the deeper parts. Although there are these basic divisions, the depths are much less in lentic waters than marine waters, and there is no equivalent of a continental shelf to delimit the littoral from the benthic zones. However, vegetation forms a good means of division. The littoral zone has vegetation of rooted plants such as grasses and lilies, and the deeper benthic parts usually have no rooted vegetation, though floating vegetation may be present.

In lotic waters there are two zones, **pool zone** where the water is relatively slow and quiet thus allowing silt settlement; and **rapids zone** where the water runs fast either through a narrow valley or over a precipice.

(c) *Terrestrial habitat*

In the land habitat, flora and fauna are so closely associated, that the same zones often apply in both plant and animal ecology. In Fig. 4, we find a map of Africa showing the major land zones based primarily on vegetation. The major zones are:

(i) Tropical forest
(ii) Savanna
(iii) Arid grassland or semi desert
(iv) Desert
(v) Montane
(vi) Chaparral

It is necessary to view terrestrial zones three-dimensionally as in the marine and freshwater habitats, in order to realize that zonal stratification also occurs. Animals are found, not only on the ground but also within the top soil and sub-soil. In montane and forest zones, animals are found at various altitudes from the ground level to the greatest heights. Hence, in the definition of the biosphere, we include all areas from the greatest depths where living things are found, to the top of the highest trees above sea level.

Physical and chemical constitution of habitats

(a) *Aquatic habitats*

For a consideration of physical and chemical properties of habitats, the marine and freshwater habitats can be taken together since their chief constituent is water. You know that the water molecule consists of two atoms of hydrogen and one of oxygen in the form of H—O—H. You are also, no doubt, familiar with some of the physical and chemical properties of pure water such as boiling point, specific heat, density, latent heat, and its solvent power.

Its power to dissolve various substances, some in large quantities and others only in minute quantities, is very important. It is because of this property that natural waters are not pure. Even rainwater is not quite pure because during its fall it dissolves carbon dioxide and minute amounts of certain nitrates and ammonia present in the atmosphere.

The following table shows the result of analysis of sea water from Lagos, and water from the Sokoto river, in Northern Nigeria. The results are expressed in parts per million, and only the main constituents are shown.

	Na	K	Mg	Ca	P_2O_5	Cl	SO_4	HCO_3	NO_3
Lagos sea water	10 550	380	1270	400	trace	18 980	2650	140	trace
Sokoto river*	8·7	2·8	7·0	32·0	20·0	6·0	trace	77·8	0·44

Table I. Comparison of constituents of sea and river water in parts/million.
(*After Holden and Green.)

The chief sources of these salts are the atmosphere and the soil, from both of which they are washed by rainwater, and then swept into rivers, inland lakes, lagoons, and the sea.

Another source of these mineral salts is the vegetation and animals which inhabit these waters. They utilize these mineral salts, and when they die their bodies become decomposed, and the salts are once more returned to the water. This is very similar to the way in which plants, when they die, fertilize the land.

The chief difference between sea water and freshwater is the concentration of salts present. The total of salts in the sea is very high compared with freshwater, and the total salt concentration reaches an average of 35 parts per thousand. This is called the **salinity** of the water. These salts have accumulated in the sea for millions of years, and because the chlorides do not seem to be used like the other salts, they have accumulated much more, thus becoming dominant. The quantity of chlorides in sea water is known as the *chlorinity* of the water. Because the ratio of the different salts in the sea remains fairly constant, the measure of chlorides (chlorinity) is often sufficiently accurate to permit the calculation of total salinity. There will be more about this in Chapter 3.

The substratum of aquatic habitats can also be considered together. They may be *sandy, muddy, or of mixed particles.* The *sandy substratum* consists of quartz particles of varying sizes. The shape and size of these particles are important, since the ability of sand to hold water depends on them.

In a typical sandy substratum, there are two layers, a *yellow layer* above and a *black layer* occurring at varying depths below the surface. The blackening of the lower layer is due to the activity of certain bac-

Habitat	Sub-habitat	Zones
MARINE	Pelagic	Euphotic Disphotic Bathypelagic Abyssopelagic Hadopelagic
	Bottom	Supratidal Intertidal Subtidal Bathyal Abyssal Hadal
FRESHWATER	Lentic	Littoral Benthic Euphotic Disphotic Aphotic
	Lotic	Pools Rapids
TERRESTRIAL		Forest Savanna Desert Montane

Table II. Summary Table of Habitats.

teria which cause the formation of iron sulphide, and the depth of this layer depends on the porosity of the sand. When the particles are porous and there is good circulation of oxygen-rich water between them, the surface yellow layer is deep and the black layer at some distance from the surface, but when porosity is poor, the black layer is closer to the surface and the yellow layer may be virtually non-existent.

A muddy *substratum* consists of finer particles of silt and organic material than a sandy bottom. Gradations between these two types of substrata are to be found, and it is difficult to draw a sharp line between them.

(b) The terrestrial habitat

In the land or terrestrial habitat, varying from swamps to mountains and desert, there are usually both a topsoil and a subsoil. Except over granite rocks and outcrops, there is always a layer of soil cover. It is this relatively thin topsoil that forms the bulk of the habitable part of the land. It consists of varying mixtures of soil particles and organic material, which in turn account for variation in porosity and related characteristics. Although the decomposing organic materials are primarily at the surface, they may be carried down into the subsoil by burrowing animals.

The study of soil has become known as *soil science*, but with the multitude of animals to be found above and in the soil there is no doubt that the ecology of soil animals is an important aspect of soil science.

Things to do

(i) Select a suitable aquatic habitat in your area and divide it into appropriate zones. Make the necessary measurements and produce a sketch-map of the area.
(ii) Devise a means for the measurement of changes in water level and depth in an aquatic habitat in your area.
(iii) Determine the depth of the surface soil in different parts of a given area of land.
(iv) Determine the depth of the 'black layer' in selected areas of intertidal zone in a lagoon.

3: Ecological factors

Definition

Any factors which are liable to cause changes in a habitat are called ecological factors. For each of the different habitats, the important factors differ, but there are a number of ecological factors which are common to all. These will be considered first.

Ecological factors common to all habitats

(a) *Rainfall*

If I were living in a temperate country or writing this account for use in temperate climates, the first factor to be listed in this chapter would have been temperature since it is such a major variable climatic factor in the temperate zone. For West Africa, I would not hesitate to consider rainfall first because it seems to be the most important climatic factor, not only for the human population in tropical areas, but for most of the other living organisms as well.

The direct effect of rainfall is that it soaks the soil, and after the soil has become saturated, the excess water flows into streams, rivers, lakes, lagoons, and thence into the sea. In West Africa, the rivers are drained into three main basins; namely, the **Chad basin,** the **Niger basin,** and **the coastal lagoons and the sea.**

For life in the freshwater habitat, rainfall is of utmost importance. Without rain, the body of water gradually dries up, and only the lung fish and some small invertebrates have developed means of survival when this happens. The former builds a mud cocoon round itself, and is able to make use of atmospheric air; whilst the latter have resting eggs which can survive dryness, and may in fact be blown about by wind. Nevertheless, the period through which they are able to survive in this way is limited; and furthermore, these animals are only a very small fraction of the total of aquatic animals.

Figures 5 and 6 show the relationship between the rainfall and the river levels in the Sokoto river, in the north west of Nigeria, and the

ECOLOGICAL FACTORS

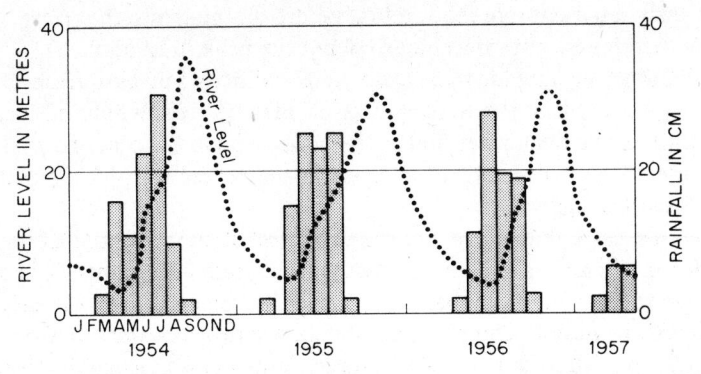

Fig. 5. Monthly rainfall and levels of Sokoto river at Birnin Kebbi from 1954–57 (after Holden and Green).

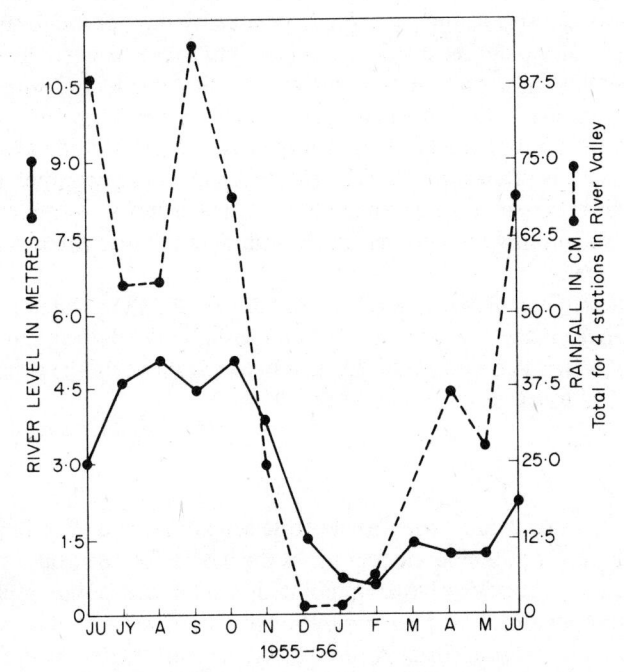

Fig. 6. Monthly rainfall and levels of Ogun river near Lagos, 1955–56.

Ogun river, in south west Nigeria. There is no doubt as to the direct relationship between river levels and rainfall in both examples.

It is interesting to note the way in which the water levels do not immediately rise at the start of the rains, due no doubt to the fact that the early rains saturate the soil first before draining into the rivers; and how the highest water level lags behind the peak in rainfall.

With marine habitats there is no danger of drying up as in freshwater. The salt content of the water, however, may be greatly reduced locally because of the freshwater flowing into the sea. On the other hand, lack of rainfall may also lead to increase in the percentage salt content of enclosed marine waters.

Terrestrial habitats too are greatly affected by rain, and although water in the soil is usually primarily associated with plants, it is also important for most animals. It should be remembered that certain animals, including almost all amphibia, are tied to water for their reproduction. Many animals of forests and grasslands must go to streams, rivers, and water holes to drink; and certain insects such as termites require a rain-soaked soil before they can start their new colonies. The swarming of termites in the evening of a rainy day, particularly in the early part of the wet season, is a familiar sight to everyone in the tropics. One wonders how many people realize that the time of swarming is not accidental, but is the most favourable time for such activity.

Measurement of rainfall with a *rain gauge,* a simple and well-known instrument, is often supervised by the department of geography in most institutions; it should be remembered that it is equally important for biologists to show keen interest in the rainfall and other climatic records for the area.

Measurement of water level in running or standing water is with a *depth gauge,* fixed at a convenient point, usually the deepest part of the body of water. A depth gauge marked in feet is shown in the foreground of the Frontispiece.

(b) *Temperature*

Reference has already been made to temperature as a very important climatic factor in temperate regions of the world. Temperatures of 30°C in summer and below freezing point in winter are commonplace in temperate regions. The *temperature range* is even wider at places far inland than in coastal areas. Although temperature variation in tropical waters is not so pronounced, it would be wrong to suppose that there is no variation worth considering. We have seasonal and diurnal variation in air and water temperature during the dry and rainy seasons and this is clearly shown in Figs. 7 and 8, which represent brackish and freshwater habitats respectively. In Fig. 7, lower temperatures are recorded during the rainy season than in the dry season, whereas the

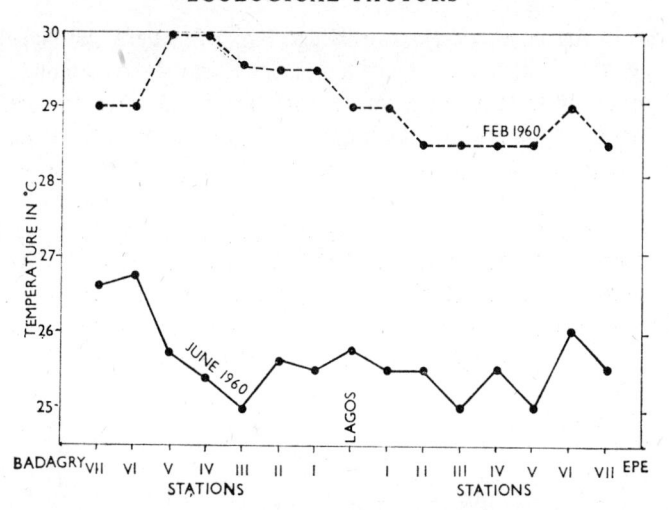

Fig. 7. Temperature variation in surface lagoon waters in 1960, between Epe and Badagry in dry (Feb). and rainy (June) seasons.

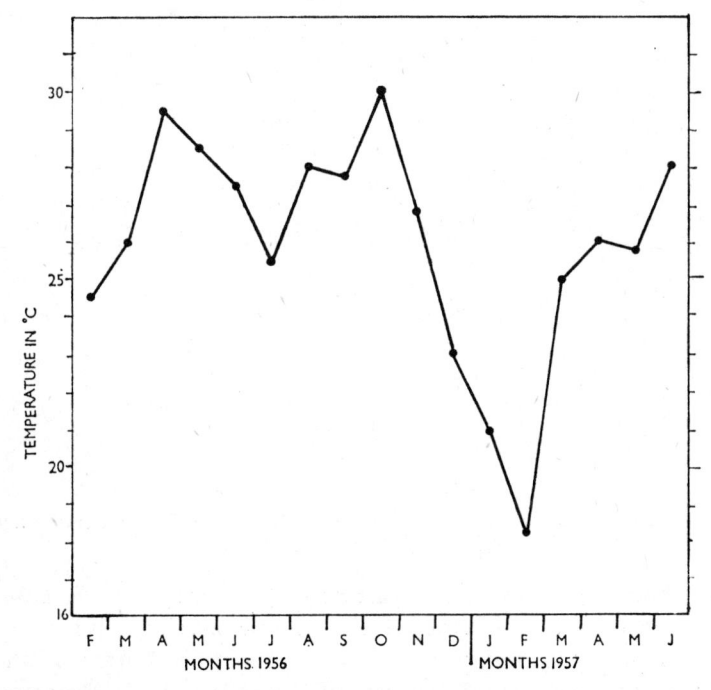

Fig. 8. Temperature variation in water of Sokoto river in 1956–57 (after Holden and Green).

reverse is the case for Sokoto river (Fig. 8), where the harmattan winds cause a sharp lowering of temperature in the dry season.

Another important temperature variation in aquatic habitats is a vertical one, temperature tending to fall with depth. At a depth of 1500 metres in tropical marine waters, the temperature is about 4°C compared with 30°C at the surface. Also in lakes, it is quite clear that there is a marked difference between the temperature at the surface and at the bottom. More important is the fact that the fall in temperature is not uniform, but that there is a sharp fall at a depth of about 2 metres in shallow lakes, so that there are two bodies of water, the one above of higher temperature than the one below (see **Fig. 9**).

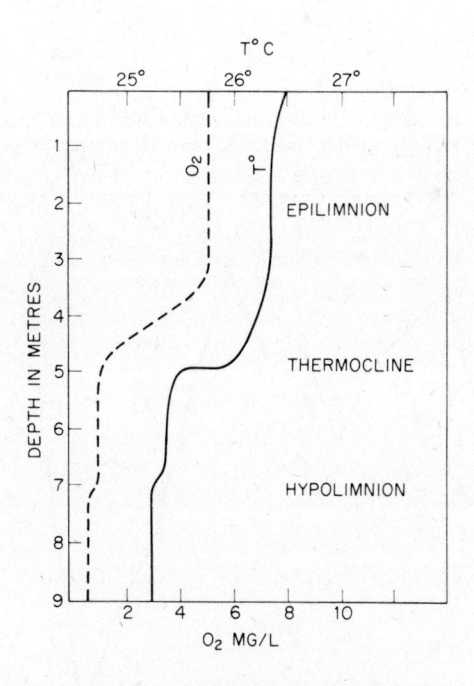

Fig. 9. Temperature and oxygen content variation between surface and deep water in Eleyeile lake, 1961 (after Imevbore).

The upper water is called the *epilimnion* and the lower one the *hypolimnion*; the narrow zone between them is the *thermocline*. This is a very important phenomenon in aquatic biology, occurring both in marine and freshwater habitats, not only in tropical waters but also in temperate waters during the warm summer months.

From the foregoing, it should not be imagined that all tropical aquatic habitats consist of two bodies of water, one sitting patiently on top of the other. Mixing usually occurs; and this may be caused by winds and storms, and could also be due to *convection currents,* a phenomenon with which you are no doubt familiar. For mixing of this type to occur, the surface water has to be of lower temperature and therefore higher density. During the night, atmospheric temperature usually falls, and this affects the surface waters so that the epilimnion becomes lower in temperature, tending to sink to the bottom. The hypolimnion does the opposite. The result is that a current is set up and an *overturn* occurs (see Fig. 10), particularly in shallow lakes.

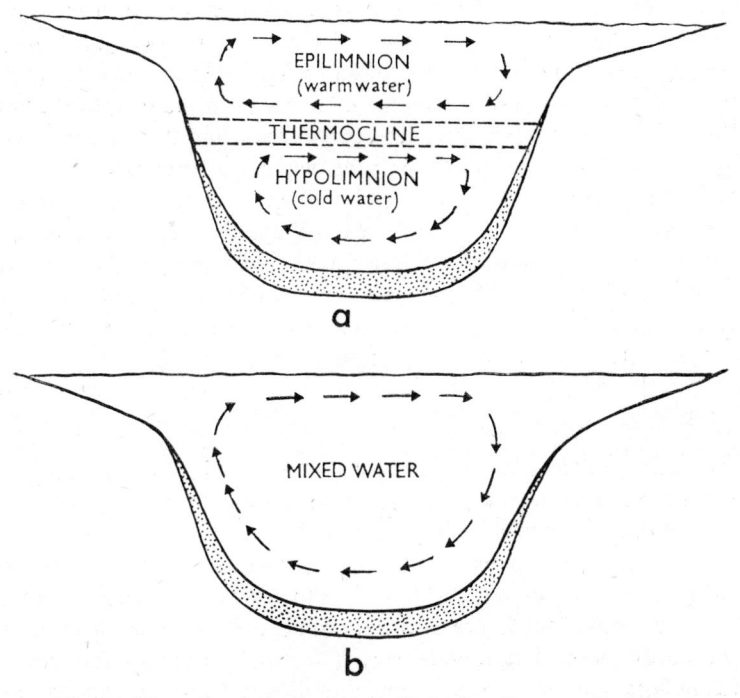

Fig. 10. Water circulation in (*a*) stratified lake, (*b*) unstratified lake.

In oceans, convection currents are very common. The *cold Benguela currents* from the south and the *Guinea currents* from the west to the east are the important oceanic currents along the West African coast; but they are only two of several to be found in the oceans of the world.

For the terrestrial habitat, both atmospheric and soil temperature are important. Seasonal and diurnal variations in atmospheric temperature have been noted earlier in this section. We also know that temperature falls with altitude, hence we can have snow-capped mountains even within the tropics. Soil temperature is less variable than atmospheric temperature; and subsoil temperature less variable than surface soil temperature.

It is probably superfluous to mention that temperature is measured with thermometers. The mercury thermometer can be used in both aquatic and terrestrial habitats, although special thermometers are often used for measuring soil temperature. For deep-water measurements a device known as a *reversing thermometer* is used. In this type of thermometer, the mercury tube just above the bulb has a loop and twist in it, and after being let down into deep water in an upright position a metal weight called a *'messenger'* is allowed to fall along the line, striking a trigger and causing the thermometer to swing rapidly upside down. When this occurs, the thread of mercury breaks, and the mercury above the kink runs into the end of the tube, which was originally the upper end but has become the 'lower' end after the reversal. The broken inverted column of mercury can be read off against a calibrated scale to obtain the temperature of the water at the time the thermometer was turned over. **Electrical thermometers or thermistors** are now in use for more advanced work, making continuous recording of temperature a simple matter. Details of construction are not relevant here.

(c) *Winds*

For both aquatic and terrestrial habitats, winds are an important climatic factor. Reference has already been made to the effect of winds on stratified water in lakes (Fig. 10), but they also play a part in the creation of water currents and waves, which are in turn important ecological factors in aquatic habitats. In terrestrial habitats such as mountain zones, winds are also important. For example areas on the windward side of a mountain may differ from those on the leeward side in flora and fauna. Measurement of direction and velocity of winds may be made with a *wind gauge.*

(d) *Light*

This is a factor of prime importance in plant ecology; because without light the fundamental process of photosynthesis cannot take place. Since animals eventually depend on plants for all their food, light is equally important to them.

Some animals feed and are active in daylight and rest at night, whilst others, particularly many carnivorous ones, especially mammals, do the reverse. In aquatic habitats many animals descend to deeper waters during daylight and ascend to surface waters when light intensity is reduced, a phenomenon known as diurnal *vertical migration.* It is presumed that these habits give certain advantages to the animals concerned, although in many cases the advantages have not been clearly understood. Some insects, especially termites, swarm at dusk and at no other time, thus taking advantage of the absence of bird predators at that time. Light as an ecological factor is even more important to animals in temperate areas because the variation in the length of daylight is far more pronounced than in the tropics. Measurements of light intensity in terrestrial habitats may be made with a *light meter* and in aquatic habitats with a *submarine illuminometer.*

(e) Pressure

This is a climatic factor of great importance in aquatic habitats, but operates in terrestrial habitats as well. The pressure of the atmosphere is reduced as we ascend from sea level, so that in mountain areas, pressure is relatively less than in lowlands. In the oceans and deep freshwater habitats, the pressure increases at the rate of one atmosphere (1.03 kg/m^3 for every 10 metres or so increase in depth. This means that at a depth of 10 000 metres the pressure would be about 100 atmospheres.

For a long time it was thought that no organisms could possibly survive in these depths because such great pressures would have profound effects on physiological and biochemical processes. Since animals have been brought up from as deep as 10 000 metres, the abyssal and hadal depths have to be accepted as truly habitable zones, to which such animals have adjusted themselves. Such animals are usually dead by the time they reach the surface, which indicates their preference for the pressure and other conditions they experience in the great depths. Conversely, surface dwelling animals die as they are exposed to the high pressures of deep water. The measurement of atmospheric pressure is by *barometers.* Below water surface, special *pressure gauges* are used.

(f) Hydrogen ion concentration (pH)

A measure of the hydrogen ion concentration *affords a measure of the acidity or alkalinity of the water* in aquatic habitats, or the soil in terrestrial habitats. pH is closely related to the amount of carbonates present, because the carbonates act as a *buffer* tending to neutralize any acidity. When enough carbonates are available, the pH tends to be neutral, with a value of approximately pH 7·0; and when no carbonates are available as buffering material the medium tends to be acid, with values of less than pH 7·0. In aquatic habitats, pH varies with salinity and oxygen content, sea water tending to be alkaline, with values of pH 8·0–8·5 in surface waters. In the soil the acid or alkaline condition may be due to a variety of factors, such as the origin of the soil, the abundance of inorganic and organic matter, and the dryness or wetness of the soil.

Of the number of methods available for the measurement of pH of water and soils the most commonly used is the colorimetric. This employs a 'universal indicator' to determine the approximate range of pH, and by using more specific indicators such as *cresol red, bromothymol blue,* etc. more accurate measurements can be made. A more convenient device for field work is the portable, battery-operated pH meter which is now commonly used.

In the past, the significance of pH changes as an ecological factor in aquatic habitats was very much exaggerated. It is now thought that the variations usually observed in sea water have comparatively little effect on most organisms.

Aquatic ecological factors

In addition to the physical factors listed above, there are a number of ecological factors which apply only to the aquatic habitats, and these will now be considered.

(a) Salinity

Salinity is a measure of the amount of dissolved salts in the water. Reference has been made to this in Chapter 2 (p. 13) and it only remains to establish the relationship between rainfall and salinity by looking at Figs. 11 and 12. In Fig. 12, the figures for rainfall are for four stations in the valley of the Ogun river.

The measurement of salinity of water is carried out by a simple chemical titration of 10 cc of the water with *silver nitrate* solution of a specific strength (27·09 g/litre), using a few drops of *potassium chromate* as indicator. The volume of silver nitrate required to change the colour from yellow to red is the salinity value of the water in parts per thousand ($S‰$). This is actually a measure of chlorides, but for practical purposes they constitute the main salts dissolved.

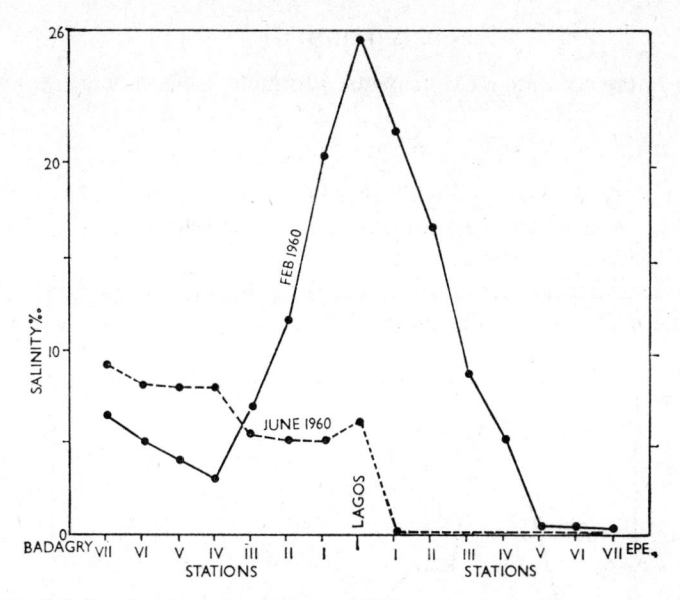

Fig. 11. Salinity of water between Epe and Badagry in dry and wet seasons, 1960.

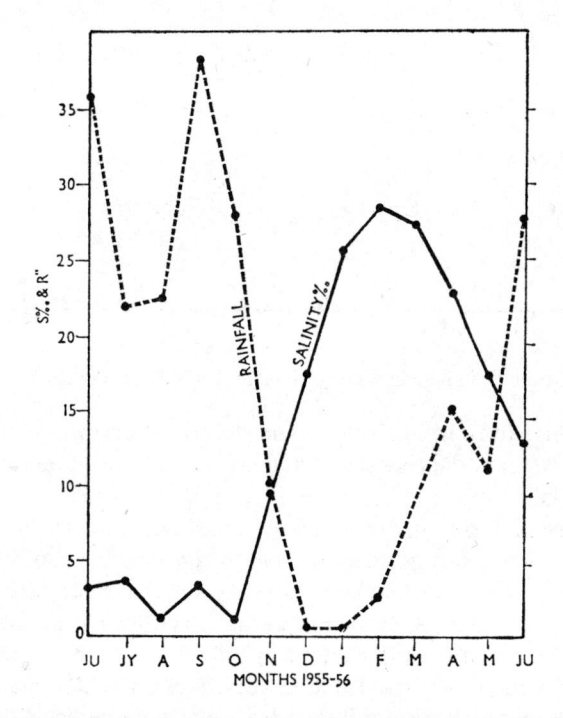

Fig. 12. Rainfall and salinity change in Lagos Harbour in 1955–56.

For more accurate measurements, a formula has been worked out as follows:

$$\text{Salinity} (S\%_{oo}) + 0.030 = 1.8050 \times \text{chlorinity} \%_{oo}$$

The variety of inorganic salts has been shown in Table I; their concentration in water varies considerably, depending on the type of soil drained by the rivers.

It seems that the first rains, after soaking the soil, pick up most of the soluble compounds from materials such as the ashes of bush fires,

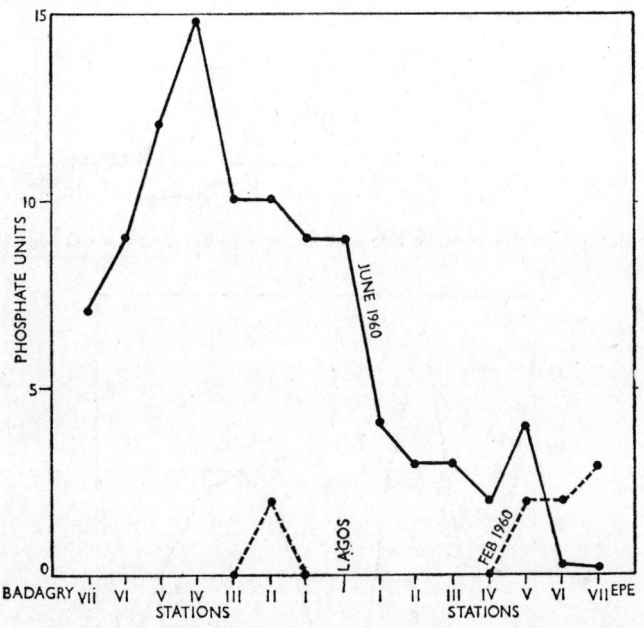

Fig. 13. Phosphate in lagoon water in 1960 in dry (Feb.) and wet (June) seasons.

animal dung, and decomposed organic debris left during the dry season, and carry them to the rivers and lagoons, so that the amount of soluble compounds is highest at this time. Figure 13 shows high concentration of phosphates during the rainy season and Fig. 14 shows high concentration of nitrite during the rainy season. These compounds appear to be rapidly used up, so much so that they sometimes appear not to be present in the water. A particular example is afforded by nitrates and nitrites, which in my experience occur only in traces in tropical lagoon water and freshwater (see Table I) yet are essential for plants. Phosphates, however, are found in large amounts compared with nitrates.

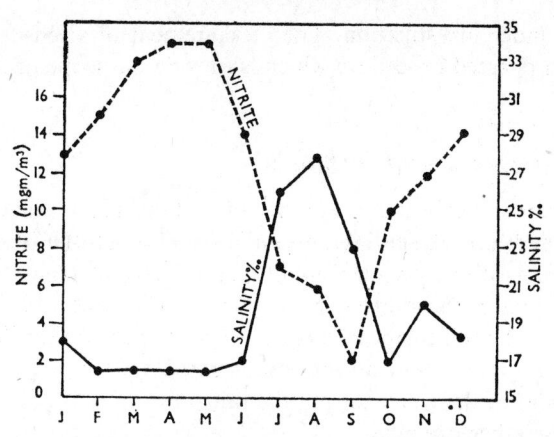

Fig. 14. Inverse relationship of salinity and nitrite abundance in estuary of Sierra Leone river (after Watts, J. C. D.).

Although they too get used up, it appears that their rate of usage is not quite as rapid as for nitrates.

There are standard methods for the measurement of the concentration of these salts in water. A bibliography for methods of measuring various ecological factors may be consulted by the teacher. A short list is at the end of this chapter.

The importance of salinity as an ecological factor is in its relation to the maintenance of osmotic balance by aquatic animals. Further explanation of this will be given in the next chapter. In general, the range of salinity in the oceans does not raise problems for most marine forms; but the sudden changes in the brackish water zone and lagoons create particular problems.

(b) Density and viscosity

The density and viscosity of a medium are factors of great biological significance in relation to the movement of the organisms in it. The density of pure freshwater is 1·00 and the density of sea water of salinity 35‰ at atmospheric pressure and 0°C is about 1·028. The specific gravity of most soft tissue is close to this, and in the open ocean it is doubtful whether the distribution of any organisms are limited by this factor. Forms which are modified for floating on the surface, such as **planktonic organisms** (explained in Chapter 4, p. 39), may be particularly sensitive to small changes in the density and viscosity of the water.

Rough measurement of density is by the use of **hydrometers.** For a more accurate determination, weigh equal volumes of pure water and the water under investigation. The measurement of viscosity requires a more complicated procedure which is outside the scope of this book.

(c) *Transparency and turbidity*

The transparency of water is another important factor, since it determines the depth to which light, essential for photosynthesis, can penetrate. It varies directly with rainfall in the freshwater habitat, transparency falling in the rainy season when a lot of salt and debris are washed from the soil by the rainwater. Measurements in the Niger, and in the Sokoto river, show an increase in *turbidity* (hence a decrease in transparency) of the water during the rains. In the coastal lagoons the variation is rather irregular.

The measurement of transparency is carried out by using a weighted disc about 10 to 15 cm in diameter, called a **Secchi disc.** It is painted white and carefully observed as it is lowered through the water. The point at which it just disappears from sight when lowered, and reappears when hauled in, can be measured on a graduated cord, and this gives a comparative measure of transparency of the water.

(d) *Currents*

Water currents which are a common feature of aquatic habitats may originate in a number of ways. In lotic freshwaters, rainfall plays an important part, causing fast currents during the rainy season when the river is flooded, compared with the trickle of slowly moving water during the dry season.

Currents in lentic freshwaters and the sea, however, are not due to rainfall but mainly due to differences in temperature between parts of the body of water in question, thus setting up **convection currents** as described under temperature (p. 21).

Currents may reduce transparency (and increase turbidity) by agitating the sediment. Currents may also cause constant shifting of the bottom if it is soft, causing a reduction in the number of fauna and flora. Currents play an important part in distribution of animals, the ocean currents in particular being important for this. For example, the Gulf Stream carries warm water up the eastern coast of North America, and the cold Benguella currents from the south spread several organisms beyond their normal limits of distribution along the coast of Southern Africa.

The measurement of the speed of water current in streams and rivers is simple. Obtain a buoyant object, such as a piece of wood, and float it down between two fixed points on the bank, timing it over the distance. If your aim is only to compare the speed for different days there is no need to measure the distance, because the times over a fixed distance will give you a sufficient basis for comparison, If, however, you wish to calculate the speed of the current, then the distance should be measured. A distance of about 100 metres in an area without obstruction should be selected. The speed may be expressed in metres per second.

(e) *Dissolved gases*

All aquatic animals require oxygen in solution and the amount available is an important ecological factor. Unlike the atmosphere where the amounts of the different gases are constant under normal conditions, there is a great deal of variation in the amount of gases dissolved in water. Oxygen, for example, is present in much smaller quantities in solution than in the atmosphere. 100 cm^3 of air would contain 20 cm^3 of oxygen, but 100 cm^3 of water at the most would contain only 1–2 cm^3 of oxygen.

The amount also varies at different depths, and the oxygen content of the epilimnion and hypolimnion is usually different (see Fig. 9). It is useful here to emphasize the importance of the 'overturn' in lakes which was mentioned earlier, because without it the hypolimnion might be permanently starved of oxygen.

Some other factors affect the amount of oxygen in solution: among these are temperature, the presence of dissolved salts, and the abundance of organic matter. The higher the temperature or salinity of the water, for example, the less its oxygen content. Biological activity affects oxygen content. As you know, the gaseous product of photosynthesis is oxygen, and when there is a bloom of vegetation in the water, if other factors are stable, there is an increase in oxygen content of the water. Winds also cause an increase in oxygen content, because, owing to the rapid movement of water, more surface is exposed to air than in quiet water and this leads to an increase in oxygen content. There are a number of methods for measuring this. Of these the Winkler method is the most widely used. In this method a solution of **manganous chloride** is added to the water sample to be analysed, followed by a solution of **sodium hydroxide** containing **potassium iodide,** which gives a precipitate of manganous hydroxide.

$$2MnCl_2 + 4NaOH = 4NaCl + 2Mn(OH)_2$$

The oxygen dissolved in the water combines with the manganous hydroxide, to form manganic hydroxide.

$$2Mn(OH)_2 + H_2O + O = 2Mn(OH)_3$$

The solution is then acidified and the potassium iodide oxidized to liberate iodine.

$$2Mn(OH)_3 + 2KI + 6HCl = 2MnCl_2 + 2KCl + 6H_2O + I_2$$

The iodine liberated is titrated against a standard solution of **sodium thiosulphate** using starch as indicator. From the result of this titration, the amount of oxygen can be calculated.

Other gases dissolved in water include **carbon dioxide, ammonia,** and **hydrogen sulphide.** The last is a poisonous gas that sometimes occurs in quantities sufficient to endanger the life of the animals. Fortunately it usually occurs only in the bottom, and animals can keep clear of this zone. If, however, there is an overturn, or due to the activity of man the water is greatly disturbed, as during 'fishing festivals', the fishes become asphyxiated and are easily caught with hand nets and hands. This is a recognized method of fishing in some parts of West Africa.

Unlike oxygen, most of the carbon dioxide which dissolves in water combines chemically with it forming carbonic acid.

$$H_2O + CO_2 \rightarrow H_2CO_3$$

The carbonic acid in turn combines with available alkalis forming carbonates and bicarbonates.

A measurement of the available carbonates is often called the **acid combining capacity** of the water. To measure it, the water is titrated against an acid, such as **hydrochloric acid;** the amount of acid required varies directly with the amount of carbonates present. **Methyl orange** is a suitable indicator.

(f) Tides and waves

Those who live close to the sea are likely to understand tides and waves more easily. At least, they know that tides are distinct from waves. My experience is that most inland people who have paid one or two brief visits to the coast are so carried away by the sight of waves beating noisily against the shore that they call it the tide. During my first visit to Lagos many years ago I was informed by the 'knowledgeable' people that the angry water was the tide.

Although waves and tides may be associated, they are two different things. If you go to a coastal city like Accra or Lagos and mark the water level against a jetty (a place where boats come alongside) or concrete pillar, and you return in about six hours, you will find that the level of the water has changed, either by falling below your previous mark or rising above it. You will see clearly that the level of the water in the sea or lagoon is changing all the time; and *it is this continuous diurnal variation in water level that is referred to as the tide*. If you take a particular day, the highest point which the water level reaches is called **high water level,** and the lowest, **low water level.** In Lagos, for example, the difference between the high water and low water level varies between about one foot and three feet. In some other parts of the world, however, especially where the sea enters a narrow estuary, the difference can be as much as 15 metres. The mouth of the river Severn in England is a good example.

The explanation for this changing in water level is based on the

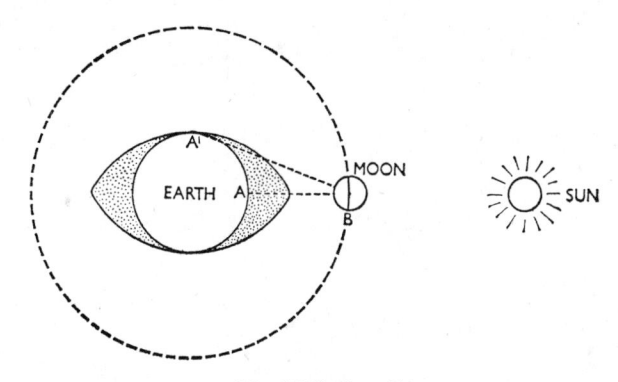

Fig. 15. Spring tides.

gravitational pull of the sun and moon on the earth, the pull by the moon being about twice that of the sun. In Fig. 15, the pull along AB is more than that along A'B.

Although the difference is small, the pull at A' causes the water to slide more easily over the earth's surface so that there is a piling of water at point A. Fig. 15 shows the sun and the moon along the same line of pull so that the maximum pull of both is exerted, thus leading to the highest high tides. This occurs twice in each month at **new moon and full moon and the resulting maximal tides are known as spring tides.** This is an unfortunate term, because the first reaction is to associate it with the season of the year known in temperate climates as spring; whereas there is no relationship at all.

When the moon is in its first or last quarter, the sun and moon form a right angle at the earth (Fig. 16). In this position, their pull is out of phase and although there is a high tide at point A, it is not as high as at spring tides. Every month, therefore, we have two periods of *spring high tides,* and two periods of *neap high tides.* Similarly, the low tide at spring tides is lower than that at neap tides.

Now, let us get back to the daily picture. For every point on the earth's surface at high tide, a point opposite to it in the other hemisphere is also at high tide. The points at right angles to them are at low tide, and all other points are at stages between the two.

Because the earth is rotating, the points of high tide (2 of them) and of low tide (2 of them) also change so that by the end of 24 hours each point would be successively at high tide, low tide, high tide, and low tide again in that order; at about 6-hour intervals. The moon, as

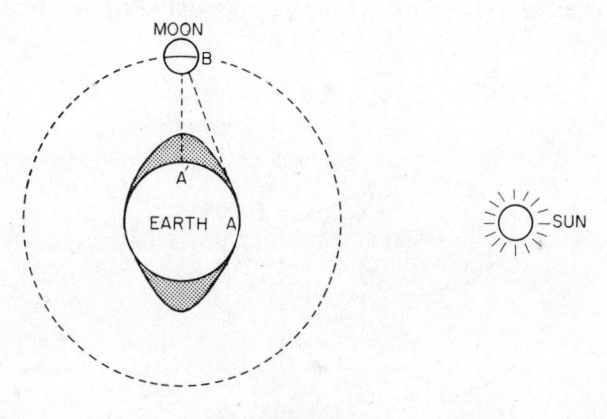

Fig. 16. Neap tides.

you know, is also moving so that it takes a little more than 24 hours to complete our daily tide cycle. Actually it takes about 24 hours 45 minutes, and because of this, times of high tide and low tide get later each day. You will find that the Port Authority in your area has what is known as *tide tables* which contain the predicted times and heights for the local high and low tides. This has been prepared primarily for the use of sailors, but nothing stops ecologists from making use of them!

Tidal movements are very important, especially for the plants and animals of the intertidal zone and estuaries. The intertidal zone is exposed twice daily. In the case of estuaries of rivers, and harbours, the sea water at high tide, because of its increased level, flows into the freshwater. Being denser, it often flows in as a form of undercurrent and may not mix very much with the freshwater for some time; but eventually at high tide there is more mixing of the water, and the whole area develops an increased salinity (see Fig. 17). In the same way, we find that at low tide the estuary or harbour becomes an area of lower salinity, especially during the rainy season. This mass movement of water as the tides change leads to quite strong currents and the inward current is

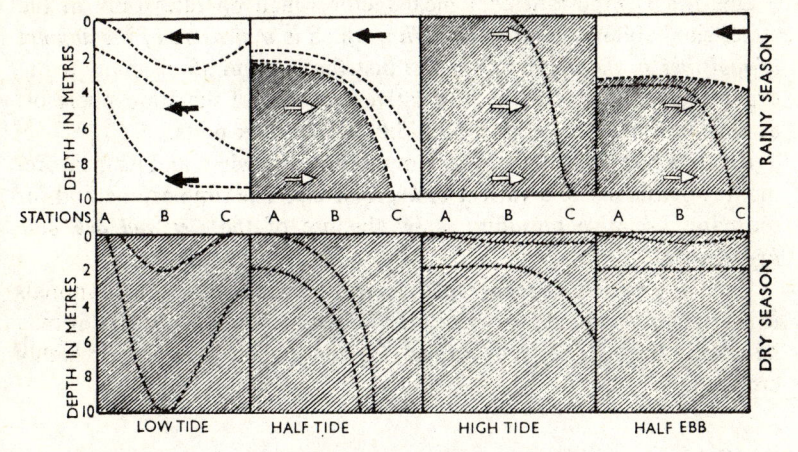

Fig. 17. Salinity changes in Lagos harbour at different depths during a tide cycle. (Water of high salinity is hatched.)

called the *flood* and the outward the *ebb*. An instrument which continuously records the variation in tide levels is a *tide gauge*.

Unlike the tide, *wave action* is difficult to define or measure as an ecological factor. Nevertheless, it is known that waves are produced by winds, and their height and period depends on the velocity of the wind, its duration, and the distance over which it is operating.

Waves are an important factor in the intertidal zone and the splash zone just above it. In the open waters they *influence aeration* and *light penetration* at the surface and considerable *mixing of water* to varying depths.

Terrestrial ecological factors

There are a number of ecological factors which operate only on land. These factors, most of which are associated with the soil, are called *edaphic factors* and are of great significance in plant ecology, since plants are the only sessile land organisms. Soil varies greatly in its *chemical composition,* its *physical composition,* its *moisture content,* and its *thickness;* and these constitute edaphic factors. This variability is reflected in the type and richness of plant life which it supports. The nature of plant life in turn affects the animal life.

We may also note that the composition of the soil may be affected directly by animals which burrow into it, such as earth worms, ants, and beetles, and by micro-organisms which hasten the decay process. In this respect, the activity of animals constitute an edaphic factor.

One other important ecological factor which operates only in the terrestrial habitat is *relative humidity,* which is *a measure of the amount of moisture in the atmosphere.* The distribution and life of many living organisms is influenced by the relative humidity of the atmosphere or, as with termites, the relative humidity within their nests.

Relative humidity varies with temperature and wind, and its measurement is by the use of a variety of *hygrometers.* The simplest method for estimating relative humidity is by the use of the *wet and dry bulb hygrometer.*

Finally, a variety of *topographic factors* may affect the life of animals in a terrestrial habitat; for example an area may be hilly or flat, it may be poorly drained or well drained, it may include a ravine or highly eroded areas.

Biotic factors

All the ecological factors so far considered are climatic, physical or chemical and are collectively called *abiotic factors.* As mentioned in Chapter 2 (p. 7) *biotic factors* are also very important when considering an environment. However, the factors of *food abundance, feeding relationships, crowding or dispersal of individuals,* and other complex factors will not be dealt with at this stage, but will be considered in Chapter 9 as part of the interrelationships of animals.

Limiting factors

We now have a list of ecological factors which are liable to vary in different habitats. Their importance for the different habitats and for particular animals within them cannot be the same. For example, a change in temperature does not greatly bother a 'warm-blooded' animal whereas it can be disastrous for a 'cold-blooded' animal. Again, in a terrestrial habitat, oxygen abundance is never an important variable factor because it is known that oxygen is always present in abundance in the atmosphere. In an aquatic habitat, however, it is all important because it is liable to a great deal of variation, depending on a number of other factors.

It is generally accepted that the life of an *organism depends on a complex of several factors, both external and internal, yet if any one of these factors became deficient (or in excess) the organism would not survive.* Any such factor is called a **limiting or critical factor** and any of the factors which have been listed in this chapter can become 'limiting' for particular animals in particular environments. The idea has grown from plant ecology in which it is known that certain mineral salts are essential for growth in minute quantities in addition to those which have to be supplied in large quantities.

The importance of recognizing a limiting or critical factor in ecological study is enormous. It enables the ecologist to pay particular attention to such factors which are, so to say, weak links in the relation of the organism with its environment.

Things to do

(i) Work out the relationship between the rainfall and the water level in a lake in your area. From a suitable map, estimate the extent of the area which is drained into the lake and find out any information about the soils of the area.

(ii) Carry out measurements of some of the various ecological factors given in this chapter.

(iii) For those who live near the sea, find some convenient place where you can measure the tidal range (difference between high tide and low tide levels) at the following times over a period of about 3 months.

New moon
1st quarter
Full moon
3rd quarter

The predicted dates for the phases of the moon may be found in a suitable calendar; and predicted times for high tide and low tide may be found in tide tables published by the Port Authority of your area. For this type of observation requiring a number of observers at different times, it is important that all concerned must agree on the exact way measurements will be carried out.

What conclusions do you reach from your observations?

(iv) Measure the temperature. Temperature is the most easily measured ecological factor. Measure temperature as follows using a Centigrade thermometer. The class should be divided into at least 3 groups with each group making independent measurements.

(*a*) In the classroom
(*b*) Outside the classroom

(c) In the open
(d) In the shade under a large tree
(e) In the shade under a shrub
(f) At soil surface
(g) At 25 cm deep in the soil
(h) At water surface
(i) At 1 metre deep in water.

For (i) a water sample can be taken using a weighted tin can (e.g. milk tin). Make sure there are two small openings to enable air to escape from one as water enters through the other. When no more air bubbles are seen on the surface, the tin is full. Discuss your results.

4: The adaptation of animals

The concept of adaptation

One of the most striking things in nature is the way most animals (and plants, for that matter) seem to be just right for their habitats. A fish is helpless and clumsy on land, but put it in water and behold the most graceful creature you can imagine darting about with effortless ease.

To the student of biology, this situation is only logical. If these animals were not fitted for their habitats, they would not be there at all. They would die. There is no doubt of the fact that animals must have the correct structures in order to survive in particular habitats and zones, and also to survive under the influence of the various ecological factors. Unless they are able to cope, they perish, and there is enough evidence of this in geological history where we find that many groups of animals which once flourished became extinct.

The characteristics which animals possess, which fit them for particular habitats, are known as ***adaptive characteristics*** and the concept is known as ***adaptation.*** Take, for example, an animal living in the intertidal zone. It becomes exposed to the air twice a day for periods of about 6 hours each if it lives well up in the zone, and submerged for the two periods of high tide. In order to survive in this intertidal zone, it must be adapted for both exposure and submergence, and you will find in Chapter 5 that many animals have in fact succeeded in doing this.

Pre-adaptation

It is now accepted by most biologists that life must have begun in the sea. There is a great deal of evidence in support of the theory. One of the most cogent is that the body fluid of animals is very close in constitution to that of sea water. Assuming that the earliest living things were simple, it is reasonable to suggest that in order to survive (which they did!) the best medium in which to live would be one with very similar constitution to their own body fluid. From these earlier organisms, more and more complicated ones which eventually found their way to freshwater and land habitats must have developed.

To be able to do this, they must have developed some characteristics which were virtually useless whilst still in the marine habitat but which served them successfully when they moved to freshwater and onto land. This type of character is called a **pre-adapted** characteristic and the concept **pre-adaptation**.

Now, no biologist can prove the theory of adaptive or pre-adaptive characteristics. To do so, he would need to have lived in prehistoric times, perhaps several million years ago when such characteristics which were useless in water became useful on land during invasion of land. Nevertheless, we find that today there are many animals which have the sort of pre-adapted characteristics similar to those which could be predicted in particular situations. There are some animals which can swim from the sea, through estuaries into freshwater and back again, even though their nearest relations cannot. A good example is the common West African sting ray *Trygon*. There are some fishes, such as the mud fish *Clarias* and climbing perch *Ctenopoma* which can wander out on land for some periods before returning to water. There are even the lung-fishes (such as *Protopterus*, previously mentioned in Chapter 3) which already have a 'lung' and can survive for weeks without water. Conversely there are land animals which have to return to water to lay their eggs because their young will only develop in water. Insects such as dragon flies and the toad *Bufo regularis* are familiar examples. All these and many others, point to the fact that the different present-day inhabitants of the major habitats have not always been there, and could only have been able to change their habitat and survive in their latest one by possessing an appropriate combination of pre-adaptive and adaptive characteristics.

There are a number of basic characteristics which a marine animal must possess, and in the same way freshwater and terrestrial animals require particular adaptations to fit them for their habitat. Let us look at these requirements one by one starting with the marine habitat.

Life in the sea

(a) *Body fluids*

We have already noted that it is best for an animal to have body fluids close in constitution to that of its habitat. **Osmosis**—the *passage of water through semi-permeable membranes*—is a process which operates not only in plants but also in animals. If the concentration of the body fluids of an animal is the same, or very close, to that of its habitat, then the rate of passage of water from outside into its body will be the same, or almost the same as in the opposite direction. In other words, there will be *osmotic equilibrium.*

In Table III you will see the comparison of the constitution of the body fluids of three marine animals representing three important phyla, the *Coelenterata, Echinodermata,* and *Mollusca,* with that of sea water. The amount of different salts in the different animals is expressed as a percentage of that in sea water.

	Na^+	K^+	Ca^{++}	Mg^{++}	Cl^-	SO_4^{--}
Sea water	100	100	100	100	100	100
Jellyfish	99	106	96	97	104	47
Starfish	100	111	101	98	101	100
Sea snail	101	114	102	101	101	98

Table III. Relationship between sea water and body fluids of marine animals (after Robertson).

Except for 47% sulphate in jellyfish, the amounts of the various salts are reasonably close to that of sea water. This is why, as was pointed out in Chapter 3 (p. 27), the small variation in salinity of ocean water does not create a problem for marine animals. It is in the brackish and fresh waters that important problems of osmoregulation arise.

(b) Respiration

The ideal respiratory organ for an aquatic animal, and in fact for all animals, is one which will enable it to absorb oxygen in solution. In land animals, the oxygen first goes into solution on a wet respiratory surface, but in aquatic forms the respiratory organ is bathed by water which contains oxygen already in solution. Such an organ is called a *gill* and is found in various forms in different groups of marine animals. It usually has a **thin surface,** and is **highly vascularized** to cope with its function of gaseous interchange (see Fig. 18). When there are no gills, the whole or part of the body surface is used as a respiratory surface.

Among aquatic animals, especially sedentary forms, it is essential to have a water current moving across the respiratory surface so that fresh oxygenated water is brought continuously to it, and water saturated with carbon dioxide is removed. **Respiratory currents,** as they are called, are set up by various methods in different aquatic animals, varying from the *use of cilia, flagella, and various types of modified appendages in many invertebrates, to muscular movements of the pharynx floor in fishes.*

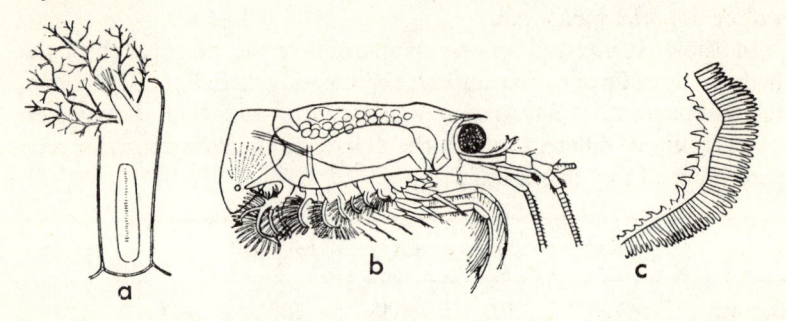

Fig. 18. Gill structure in (*a*) parapodium of Polychaete worm, (*b*) limbs of Crustacea, and (*c*) gill arch of Dogfish.

(*c*) *Locomotion*

From the point of view of their means of locomotion, marine animals consist of three types. There are those which can swim actively from place to place (*nekton*), with the aid of powerful locomotory organs, and those which simply drift about in the water, although they do carry out some limited locomotion (*plankton*). The third group are those which are either fixed to the substratum, or move only slowly over its surface (*benthon*). Among the plankton, various devices are employed to keep the animal afloat and enable it to carry out vertical movements from surface to deeper waters and *vice versa*. The development of *ciliated bands, spines, oil droplets,* and other similar devices are used. This is discussed further, with appropriate examples, in Chapter 5.

Nektonic organisms have a variety of appendages modified for *swimming,* such as jointed appendages among the crustacea, *fins* and associated structures among fishes, and a *siphon, an organ of jet propulsion* (pumping water out forcibly to cause movement in the opposite direction) among a group of molluscs called the *Cephalopoda*. It is ironical to think of the proverbial saying 'as slow as a snail', when in fact, some members of the same phylum as the snails, namely the cephalopods, are among the fastest animals in the sea!

Benthonic organisms move slowly over the substratum or may not move at all. A majority of slow-moving benthonic organisms belong to the PHYLUM *Mollusca* (e.g. snails of various types), and the PHYLUM *Echinodermata* (e.g. starfishes). In the first, use is made of the gliding muscular *molluscan foot*, and in the second, the numerous *echinoderm tube feet* are used.

Fixed and tube-dwelling benthonic organisms are found in the PHYLUM *Coelenterata* (e.g. hydroids and sea anemones), the PHYLUM *Annelida* (e.g. tubiculous worms), the PHYLUM *Arthropoda* (e.g. barnacles), the PHYLUM *Urochordata* (e.g. sea squirts) and the PHYLUM *Echinodermata* (e.g. sea lilies). To compensate for lack of movement in these animals, they usually develop a form of *radial symmetry*, as distinct from *bilateral symmetry* of active animals. They have long *tentacles* which they use in their feeding processes, or some richly ciliated surface for drawing a water current, bearing plankton food, through their bodies. Those of the latter group are called *ciliary feeders*.

(d) Protection

Protection from enemies and from the effects of any adverse physical and chemical changes in the environment is essential, especially for animals which are fixed, such as sea anemones, hydroids, annelids, molluscs, and others mentioned above which cannot escape by swimming. Various adaptations are to be found.

(i) *Digging in*, as in various molluscs, and in the sand star *Astropecten*.
(ii) *Withdrawal of the whole body into a shell or tube,* as in many molluscs and various tubiculous annelids.
(iii) *Withdrawal of tentacles and enclosure of water* in body cavity as in sea anemones and barnacles.
(iv) *Holding fast,* as in many molluscs and echinoids.

In fact, very few marine animals wait to be picked up on a sandy or rocky beach, and you will find that a spade, sieve, and scalpel are essential items for collection on the sea shore.

Nektonic organisms have their own protective mechanisms. Protective coloration by *breaking the outline* with horizontal or vertical stripes is a common method, as in the fish *Eques lanceolatus* (Fig. 19 (a)). Some develop structures which make them resemble *other objects* within their surrounding, for example the sea dragon *Phyllopteryx eques* resembles a sea weed, and the pipe fish *Syngnathus* looks like a blade of sea weed. Cephalopods have developed a method of *ejecting a black substance* into the water to provide a screen whilst they escape.

Planktonic organisms on the whole are rather helpless and have no definite protective features, although their *transparency* may be regarded as protective, since their predators will see through them. A protective method adopted by some coelenterates, such as the jelly fishes, is the possession of powerful stinging organs.

Fig. 19 (*a*) Protective coloration in the fish *Eques lanceolatus* (after Cott).
(*b*) The sea dragon: *Phyllopteryx eques* (after Cott).

(e) Reproduction

Production of a large number of *small eggs which are adapted for floating* is common in many members of the marine habitat. There are also those whose eggs are laid on the sea floor. An important adaptation of marine animals is *external fertilization* for which the marine medium is ideal, since the gametes have cytoplasm similar in concentration to that of sea water. Early development as a *pelagic larva* is almost universal, and in the case of sedentary animals this enables a distribution of the species over a wide area so that intensive competition within the species, which would result from overcrowding, is avoided.

Life in freshwater

(a) Body fluids

It has previously been pointed out that the most important difference between marine and freshwater habitats is that the concentration of salts in solution in freshwater is comparatively very small. Therefore the osmotic pressure of the medium is low, whereas most of the animals in freshwater continue to maintain body fluids similar to that of marine animals. Consequently, the salt content of their body fluids is much higher than in the habitat. Because of this, more water tends to pass into the animal than out of it, and more salts pass out, unless there was some process to compensate for this in order to achieve equilibrium.

If there were no compensatory processes, the animal would be bound to expand beyond limits and burst after some time. This explains why some groups of animals have not found their way to freshwater at all. Of the twenty major groups (*phyla*) at present recognized by zoologists, all have marine representatives and at least four are found *only* in the sea. Fewer groups are represented in freshwater and on land. Those which have flourished in freshwater have developed means of regulating the osmotic movements of water; a process known as *osmoregulation.* This has been achieved by the development of a variety of osmoregulatory organs.

Two well-known microscopic animals, *Amoeba* and *Paramaecium*, may be taken as examples. Both are freshwater animals, and you will remember that one of their important *organelles* is the contractile vacuole. The excess water accumulates in the contractile vacuole and is then pumped out when full. One of the most fascinating things you can watch under a microscope is *Amoeba* or *Paramaecium* getting rid of its excess water in this way. It is true that the contractile vacuole is partially excretory in function, but for freshwater animals there is no doubt that the primary function is to get rid of excess water.

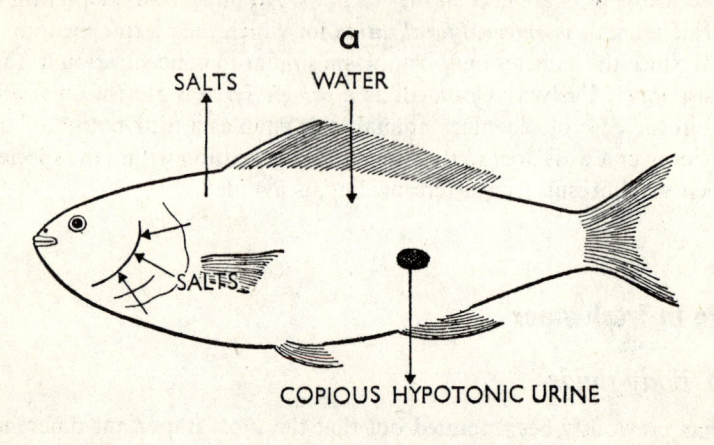

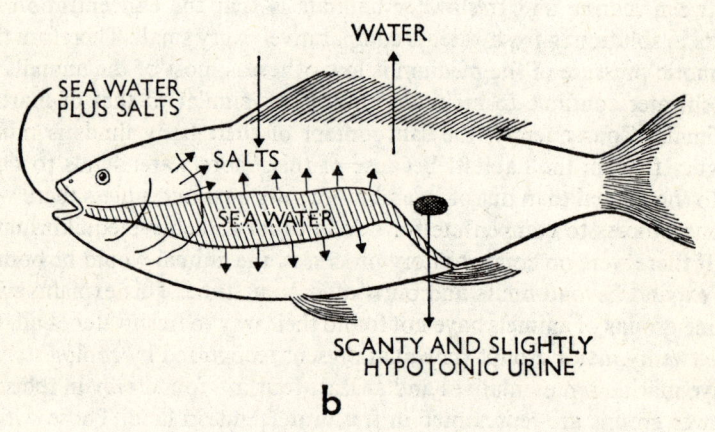

Fig. 20. Osmotic currents in freshwater and marine Fishes.

In animals more complicated than *Amoeba* and *Paramaecium*, contractile vacuoles are not present, but there are organs which perform the same function. Among crustacea, the osmoregulatory organ is the **antennal gland** and among vertebrates the **kidney** performs this function.

In some freshwater animals, the osmotic concentration of their body fluids has become greatly reduced, so that the amount of excess water which passes in is much less than it would have been if the osmotic concentration had remained the same as in marine animals. In the bivalve *Anodonta*, for instance, the concentration is only about 4 to 5% of that of marine animals; also in the prawn *Palaemon serratus* the blood is less concentrated than sea water. However, this is still higher than the concentration of salts in freshwater, and without adequate osmoregulatory organs 'death by bursting' would only be delayed and not avoided. In addition to osmoregulatory organs, many freshwater crustacea minimize water exchange by having an outer covering almost completely impermeable and restricting their surface that may be necessary for exchange between blood and water to the barest minimum.

With the necessary and adequate osmoregulatory organs, things look well organized for both marine and freshwater animals; but what happens should an animal attempt to migrate from sea into freshwater and *vice versa*? Such a journey would involve some life in brackish water, a habitat (or sub-habitat) with its own peculiar problems for the animals that live therein.

Brackish waters are usually defined as waters with salinity of between 30‰ and 0·5‰, and are usually found in estuaries and lagoons where salinity changes rapidly with the tides. Further adaptations are required for life in such water; and details of this will be considered as an introduction to the fauna of brackish waters in Part II. It may be noted that the fauna consists of three groups—marine animals which can tolerate low salinities, freshwater animals which will tolerate moderate salinities, and the true brackish water animals which are not found in either sea water or freshwater.

A few animals will, however, tolerate anything from the highest salinities to freshwater. One such animal is the prawn *Leander longirostris*, and among the copepods *Acartia clausii*, which is one of the most common copepods in tropical lagoons, is probably able to do this. Those animals which are able to tolerate a wide range of salinity in their habitat are said to be **euryhaline;** others which will tolerate no salinity changes are said to be **stenohaline.**

(b) *Other characteristics of freshwater animals*

In other respects, such as in **respiration, locomotion, protection,** and **reproduction,** the needs of the freshwater animal are very similar to those of the marine animal; and adaptations similar to those listed for marine animals have been evolved.

There are some characteristics, however, such as **the ability to tolerate low oxygen concentration, development of drought-resistant eggs, nest**

building and **various forms of parental care** which are displayed by many freshwater animals, but not by marine animals.

Life on land
(a) Body fluids

On land, the problem is not one of being flooded with water, but that of water loss from the body. One is as serious as the other, since the end result is the same, death! Any surface which is exposed to the atmosphere is liable to lose water in the form of water vapour, the rate of water loss depending on **temperature, relative humidity,** and **the animal's surface area.**

The main method employed by animals in the terrestrial habitat to prevent water loss is the development of an **exoskeleton** which envelops the body. This is the method adopted by the arthropods in which the exoskeleton comprises a stout **cuticle.** Needless to say, they are the most successful terrestrial animals. Among molluscs, the exoskeleton is a **shell,** into which the animal can withdraw completely if necessary, sealing itself off with a layer of secreted mucus or other material. Among vertebrates the treatment is less drastic, although some reptiles such as crocodiles and tortoises have a thick exoskeleton. In other vertebrates there is only a **stratified epithelium,** with a dead outer layer, which in turn may be covered by feathers as in birds, or hair as in mammals. All these reduce water loss to a great extent.

A source of water loss is through the osmoregulatory organs, but loss is very much reduced by efficient **tubules,** which are able to reabsorb the water from the waste products, leaving a dry final product to be voided through the cloaca. Such are the **malpighian tubules** in insects, and the **renal tubules** in vertebrate animals. In certain land animals, such as some desert vertebrates, the **Bowman's capsule** of the renal unit is entirely lost, in order to reduce water loss even further.

Generally, terrestrial animals without any form of exoskeleton, or with a thin cuticle, such as the earthworms, confine themselves to burrows or live under stones and leaves; only emerging when the surroundings are wet enough. In burrows or similar situations, humidity is usually high and loss of water thereby reduced.

(b) Respiration

Two contrasting methods have been developed in the two largest groups of terrestrial animals, the **tracheal system** among terrestrial arthropods

THE ADAPTATION OF ANIMALS 47

and the *lung* in terrestrial vertebrates. Both methods emphasize the necessity to enclose the respiratory surface so that loss of water from this essentially thin and wet surface is reduced to the barest minimum. Tracheal tubes are lined with cuticle, except for the actual area of gaseous interchange which is within intracellular tracheoles and tracheal end cells. The area of gaseous interchange in the lungs of vertebrates is also well protected and infolded. In addition, in both insects and vertebrates, *closing mechanisms* may be developed, to reduce further the loss of water under more difficult conditions.

(c) *Locomotion*

Problems of locomotion on land are different from those of aquatic

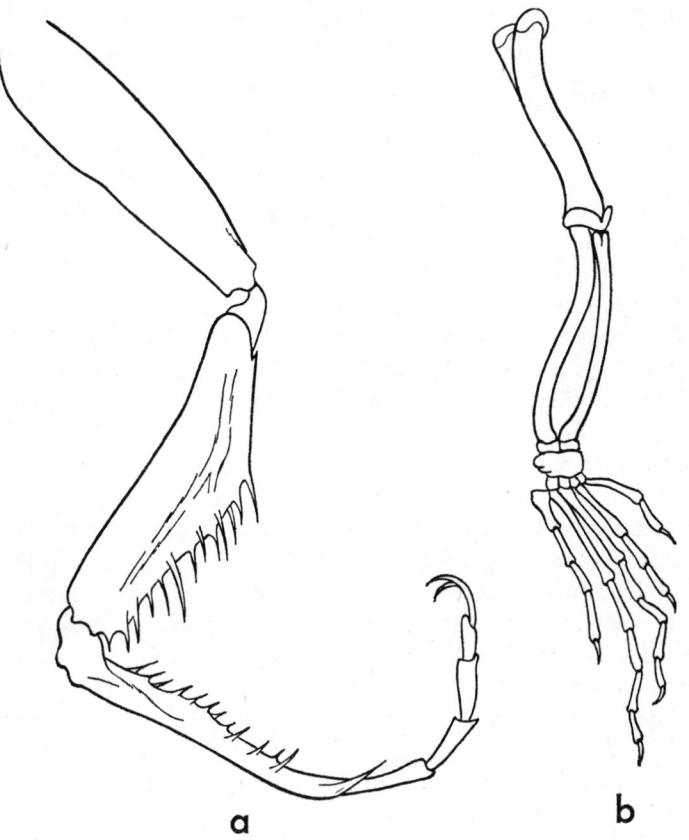

Fig. 21. The jointed limb and pentadactyl limb in (*a*) *Mantis* and (*b*) *Agama*.

animals. In water, the body of the animal is buoyed up by the water, but on land the animal has to support its body off the ground. The two main groups of terrestrial animals have again become adapted to cope with the problem in different ways, by the development of the *jointed limb* among arthropods and the *pentadactyl limb* among terrestrial vertebrates.

In principle, these limbs are similar and have been modified for *running, jumping, crawling, climbing,* and *digging* in both groups. Flight has also been achieved in both groups by different methods, by the development of a *cuticular membrane in insects,* while *feathers* in birds and a *skin membrane* in bats provide the necessary wings.

Only among the lowly earthworms has locomotion by the use of continuous sheets of circular and longitudinal segmented muscles, with body fluids providing a 'hydrostatic skeleton', been retained.

(*d*) Protection

Various methods are used. Apart from being able to fly, run, hop, crawl, or dig away from danger, among terrestrial animals several devices of protective coloration are to be found. Although protective coloration is exhibited by aquatic animals (see p. 42), it is in terrestrial animals that most study of its significance in the life of the animals concerned has been conducted.

The most common method of protective coloration adopted by animals is to resemble their background so that a prospective predator will find it difficult to spot them. This is known as *cryptic* or *concealing* coloration. Some animals go even further and are capable of changing their colour patterns to simulate a variety of backgrounds. In this respect, the saying, 'changing like a chameleon' immediately comes to mind in view of the highly exaggerated colour changing ability attributed to this animal. For a long time, I was under the impression that the chameleon was capable of 'weaving the pattern of dress' worn by an on-looker; and during my first close encounter with a chameleon I expected it to turn white on one part, and blue on the other, thus copying the colours of my school uniform! Even today, I hear school children looking at chameleons in the zoo expressing their utter disappointment at the inability of the animal to perform this feat. I also feel embarrassed when I see others who convince themselves that it has in fact changed its colours as expected! The fact is that colour change in the chameleon is not induced by the dress of an on-looker however colourful this dress may be! Colour change is induced by the general surroundings, and the range of change which is possible is limited. It can change from almost colourless to yellow, yellowish green, brownish green, or almost black, and the shades vary with the general surroundings and the temper of the animal. For example, when there is much green vegetation it is predominantly dark green, whereas when out of such surroundings it tends to be light green, yellow, or pale yellow. When angry, it has a very dark green colour; or may become almost black.

Animals may also change their colour, though less dramatically, with age. For example some young birds have a colour similar to the surroundings of their nest, but later develop an adult plumage which is very different, and may or may not be concealing.

Another method of achieving cryptic coloration is by **breaking the outline** of the body as in the zebra, shown in Fig. 22. Alternating parallel bands of dark and light colours, be they horizontal or vertical, have an effect of obscuring the outline of the animal.

Fig. 22. Protective coloration in the zebra *Equus zebra.*

For effective use of all forms of cryptic coloration, it is essential that the animals have an appropriate behavioural adaptation, namely, an ability to remain almost motionless for adequate periods. This may be followed by a sudden dash for safety. Anyone who has attempted to spot a tree quirrel will understand how effective this adaptation can be.

Sometimes animals, instead of having cryptic coloration, have just the opposite. They have bright colours called **aposematic** or **warning** colours. These colours are not protective by themselves without an appropriate behavioural adaptation. This may consist of an aggressive pose, or a secretion of distasteful, odious, or poisonous substances which the predator associates with the colours. There is a common analogy in human experience. When one picks up a millipede or caterpillar and it immediately passes its faeces on one's hands, there is a tendency to avoid picking up such animals in the future as the animal is immediately associated with the unpleasant experience.

A third type of protective coloration known as *mimetic coloration* is found in animals which have aposematic colours but do not have the appropriate behavioural adaptation associated with it in other animals with similar, but genuine aposematic colours. To put it more bluntly, they are 'fakes'; but nevertheless, mimetic colours are known to have a protective value in nature. A familiar parallel, again in human experience, is the fear which most people have for insects with a bee-like or wasp-like appearance; such insects are mere mimics, but they receive the same treatment as the bees and wasps.

Finally, we have *flash coloration,* when an animal which is cryptically coloured when at rest displays a bright colour when moving. A good example is in those grasshoppers whose fore wings are cryptically coloured whereas the hind wings, which are exposed only at take off, are brightly coloured and could 'surprise' a prospective predator. A few terrestrial animals adopt a *protective armour* as in the tortoises; and some others the development of *lethal organs of offence;* various examples, such as the development of large *spines, horns, claws,* and *teeth* are to be met in terrestrial mammals, while *poison glands* as protective lethal organs are often to be found for example in snakes, centipedes, and scorpions.

(e) Reproduction

The methods of reproduction employed in aquatic habitats are completely unsuitable on land. Terrestrial animals have therefore adopted entirely different methods. Eggs, instead of being many, small, and with little yolk, are few, large, and yolky, leading to the development of what is called a *cleidoic egg,* in which sufficient yolk is stored for the development of the embryo. Fertilization *instead of being external must be internal* to avoid drying of the gametes, and to make this possible the male and female must copulate; for this purpose, the male usually develops some means of holding the female and an *intromittent organ* for introducing the spermatozoa into the genital ducts of the female. Internal fertilization may be followed by internal development during which the developing embryo obtains all its needs from the mother as in mammals.

Survival of the fittest

I have attempted in this chapter to present the problems which confront animals in the different habitats, and the various ways in which they have become adapted to deal with these problems. It should not be expected that every animal will show all the adaptations that have been mentioned in this chapter for each particular habitat. However, most will show all these adaptations and some may even show more. Since only the best adapted will survive enough to reproduce, the poorly adapted are quickly eliminated and the survivors tend to become even better adapted. In some instances, scientists do not understand how certain animals manage to survive in some particular environments. Take for instance the animals living at a depth of 10 000 metres in the sea. How do they stand the fantastic pressure of 1000 atmospheres obtaining at such a depth? Or consider an insect larva attached precariously to the face of a waterfall, the water tumbling over it at high speed all the time, and yet it manages to feed and carry out all its normal life processes. How does it manage to do this? No one really knows. What we can say, however, is that these animals do survive, and to survive they must be adapted in some way to live under those conditions. Adaptation is a fundamental truth at the very centre of biological study, and it is closely bound up with the survival and evolution of living things. Indeed Darwin's *theory of natural selection* which seeks to explain the evolution of life is based on precisely this concept.

In Part II, I shall deal with the local animals of West Africa which are found in the different habitats, whose characteristics and basic adaptive requirements have now been considered.

Things to do

(i) Examine specimens of polychaete, prawn, and fish and study the structure of the gills.
(ii) Compare the jointed limb of an anthropod with the pentadactyl limb of a vertebrate.

Part II: Animal species ecology

5: The marine and lagoon animals—demersal forms

In the previous chapters, habitat and environment have been defined, and the adaptations which animals require in different habitats have been described. In this and the following chapters, a survey of the fauna of West Africa will be made to provide suitable examples of the habitats and adaptations already studied.

Nomenclature

The use of some English common names of animals has been a nightmare to many African students because the origins of the names are not often clear. I remember being asked as a student about the **lug worm.** I could not even guess what it was, because this was no description of the marine worm *Arenicola marina* which bears this name. Sometimes, however, common names are so descriptive that they are a useful aid to remembering the characteristics of the animal concerned. In the following chapters, therefore, common names of animals will be used when they are descriptive. They will also be accompanied by the Latin names if they are known. This is no attempt to be pedantic. The best way to refer to an animal is to give its full scientific name so that there is no possibility of confusing it with any other.

As for local names, these are bound to vary considerably in different parts of West Africa. Not only would they differ with the different languages but they may also differ with the different dialects. In view of this, local names are omitted completely.

Supratidal fauna

As you already know, the supratidal zone is not really aquatic but terrestrial. The animals which inhabit it therefore require to be adapted primarily for terrestrial life. This is most necessary for sessile animals, such as barnacles; or slow-moving ones, such as snails. For those which can move fast, or dig down to the level of the water table, there is no necessity to be fully terrestrial as they can survive by leading an amphibious life.

Such amphibious life is well exemplified by two animals commonly found in the supratidal zone of our coasts. On any sandy beach, two common crabs, the **sand-crab**, *Ocypoda africana*, and the **ghost-crab**, *Ocypoda cursor*, are to be found. They are both amphibious, living in burrows up to two feet deep. They may be seen darting into their burrow or into the water as they are approached. *Ocypoda* possesses gills like other aquatic animals, making use of oxygen in solution whilst in water; but it is also equipped with a spongy structure which functions

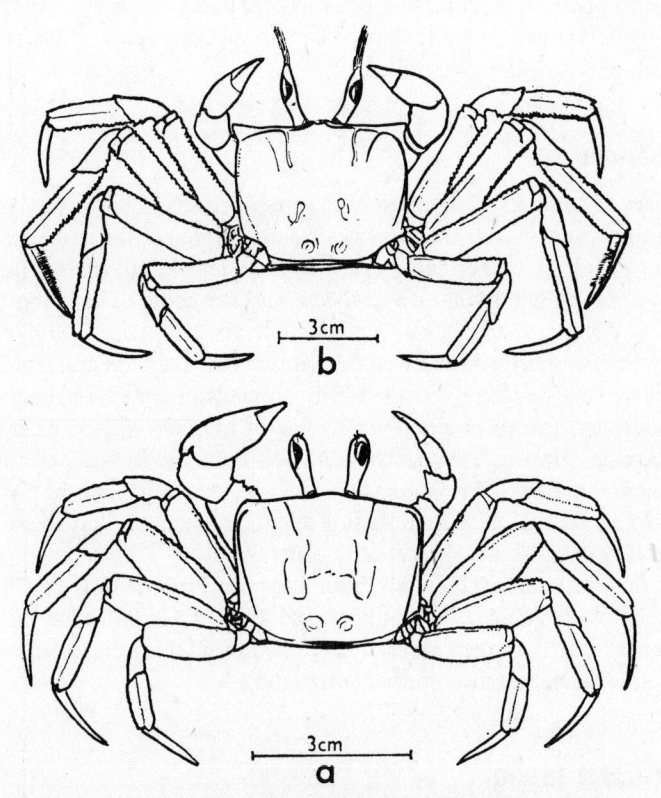

Fig. 23. Marine supratidal fauna of sandy beach (after Monod).
    (*a*) *Ocypoda africana* (sand crab)
    (*b*) *Ocypoda cursor* (ghost crab)

as a lung when out of water. It is interesting to note that it cannot remain indefinitely on land or in water. For example, if immersed in water for over 24 hours, it drowns. This shows that the amphibious nature, an ideal characteristic of the supratidal zone, is a compulsory or obligate feature.

For further examples of animals of the supratidal zone, we have to turn to a rocky shore. Unfortunately (or is it fortunately for sea bathers!), most of the West African coastline is one long sandy beach except for short breaks in Ghana and Cameroun. In Nigeria, for example, there are only artificial rocky shores in the form of harbour breakwaters which, on a modest scale, provide a variety of animals similar to those found on the natural rocky shores of Ghana.

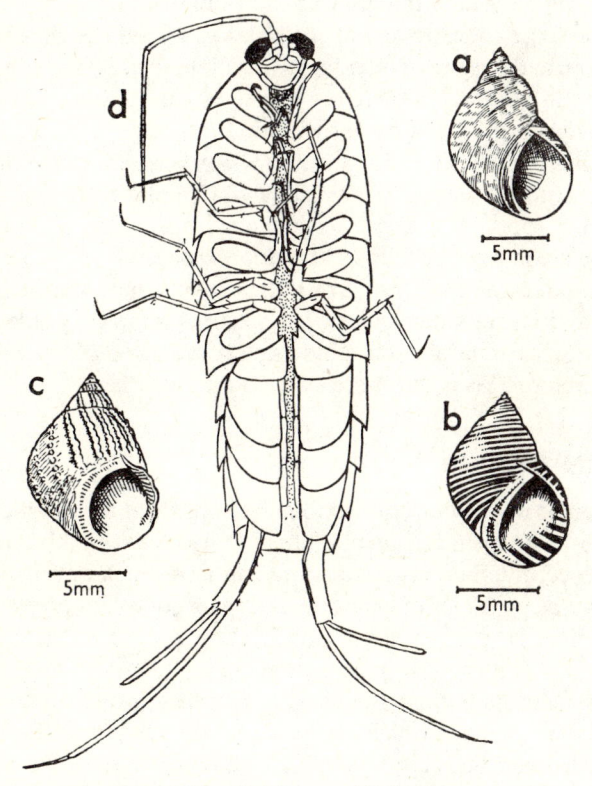

Fig. 24. Supratidal fauna of rocky shore.

(a) *Littorina punctata*
(b) *Littorina cingulifera*
(c) *Tectarius granosus*
(d) *Ligia gracilipes*

One of the dominant animals to be found in the supratidal zone is a small snail commonly known as a *periwinkle*—but more precisely *Littorina punctata* (the Latin name is clearly more meaningful, describing the spots on the shell of the male). This animal is well adapted for terrestrial life, possessing a type of lung somewhat similar to that found in the giant land snail *Achatina* with which you are probably familiar. The life history of *L. punctata* has not been studied, but in many parts of the world littorinids of the supratidal zone have been studied, and it is reasonable to expect that *L. punctata* will possess similar characteristics. In Europe, for example, the equivalent species is *Littorina neritoides*, mentioned in many European text books.

Despite their general adaptation for terrestrial life, animals of the supratidal zone require spray from the sea for their survival. As proof of this, it will be noticed that they are only found on the seaward side of the rocks. There is evidence that the water spray reduces the danger of desiccation, and in spite of internal fertilization, their young still require to develop in water. It is therefore necessary that at some appropriate high tide the eggs or larvae are shed into the water.

Two other molluscs in this zone, but which spread into the intertidal zone, are *Littorina cingulifera*, which is very similar to *L. punctata* but without the spots, and *Tectarius granosus*, which has a rough shell unlike the smooth grey shells of the *Littorina* species.

A non-molluscan member of this zone is an isopod crustacean that can stay away from water for long periods. It is completely independent of water for its reproduction, possessing a brood pouch in which the young develop. This is the shore slater *Ligia gracilipes*.

Intertidal fauna

It has been previously mentioned that the animals of the intertidal zone require to be adapted for aquatic life to carry them over the period of submergence, and must also possess adaptations which will enable them to combat the problems of exposure during low tide. The greatest needs of such animals are organs for respiration, and protection from desiccation. The position of a particular animal in the intertidal zone depends on how far its adaptations for dealing with these problems have been perfected. The animals which are best adapted are usually found high up the intertidal zone, close to the high water mark. In such a position, they may be submerged for only short periods at high tide, but they are well adapted to survive in spite of the long periods of exposure. On the other hand the least adapted for intertidal life are to be found low down

Plate I. Life on the rhizophore of *Rhizophora racemosa*
(a) Stilt roots of *Rhizophora*
(b) *Balanus pallidus* (large) below, and *Chthamalus estuarii* above
(c) *Littorina angulifera* above, and *Gryphaea gasar* below
(d) Tubes of *Mercierella enigmatica*

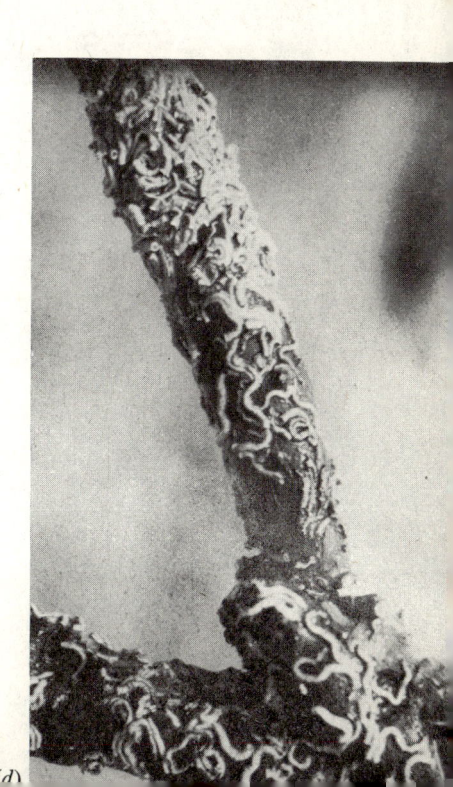

Plate II.
Kingfisher, Lagos

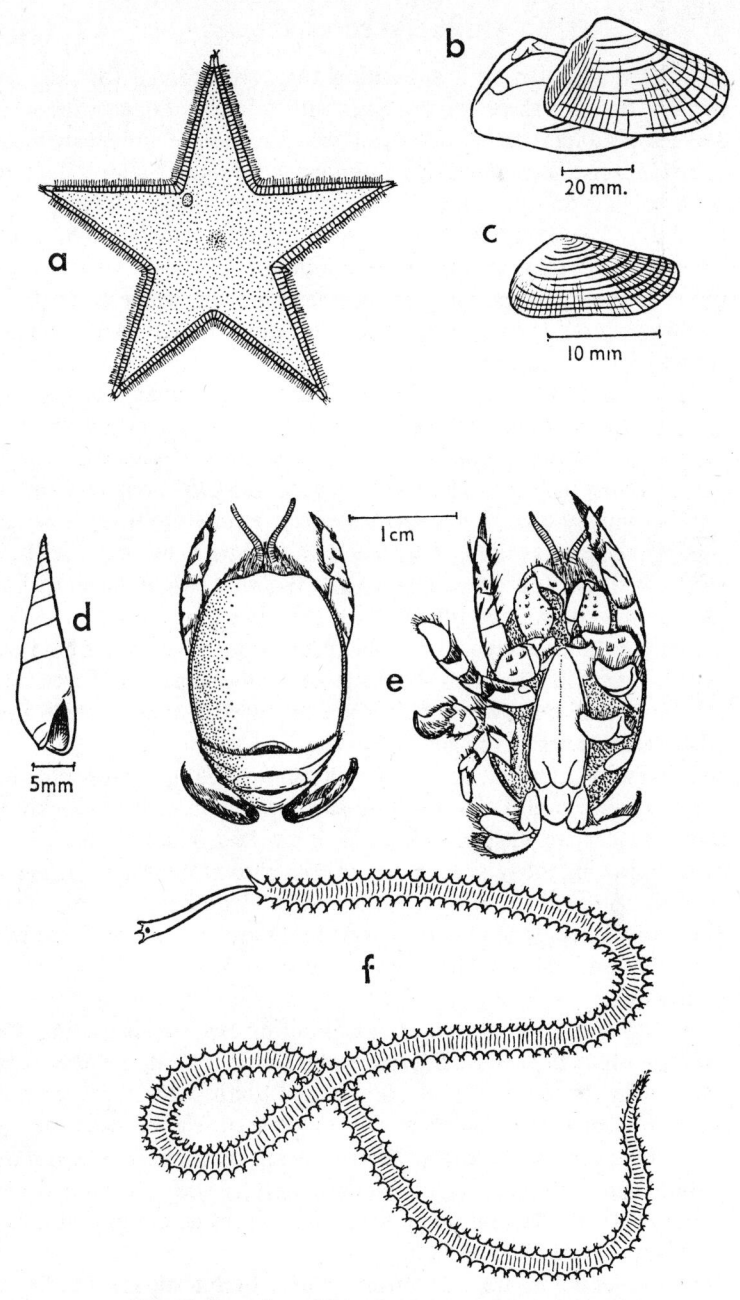

Fig. 25. Some intertidal animals of a sandy beach.

(a) *Astropecten irregularis*
(b) *Donax rugosus*
(c) *Donax pulcherrimus*
(d) *Terebra micans*
(e) *Hippa cubensis*
(f) *Glycera sp.*

within the zone, In such a position they are exposed for only short periods. Between these two extremes will be found animals with varying degrees of adaptation, so that we have a zonation of animals within the intertidal zone. *Zonation* is a well-known concept in ecological study of both animals and plants, and it is explained further on page 78.

To avoid desiccation, animals adopt various methods. On a sandy or muddy intertidal zone the most common is for the animals to dig into the sand or mud; some withdraw into their burrows as the water recedes, and hence it is common at low tide to see the intertidal zone dotted with several burrows and worm casts.

The starfish *Astropecten* is one of the largest animals of our sandy beaches which can even be seen from a distance. The others are not so easy to see, partly because they are small and partly because they are coloured like the sand. The bivalve *Donax rugosus* is not very common but the smaller *Donax pulcherrimus* may occur in thousands within a square metre of sand, as does *Terebra micans*. These molluscs have a specialized foot for active digging into the sand, while the starfish uses its hundreds of pointed tube feet for the same purpose.

Among the crustacea, the mole crab *Hippa cubensis* is found as an active digger in the intertidal zone of sandy shores, and among the inhabitants of burrows, annelids are the most common, chief among which are species of the genus *Glycera*.

Within the intertidal zone of a rocky shore, adaptation for burrowing can hardly be useful. To avoid desiccation the animals must withdraw into a protective shell or hide in rock crevices. The first method, that of withdrawing into a shell, is not restricted to molluscs, as the mention of shell may tend to suggest, but is adopted by other animals especially **barnacles.** During the period of exposure, some water is enclosed within the shell, and this enables the normal aquatic form of respiration to continue.

An important activity which ceases during exposure is feeding. Those animals which depend on filtering water for their food, the *filter feeders*, can clearly no longer feed while exposed to air. Others which feed on vegetation or other animals are also unable to feed because the movements involved would lead to loss of the enclosed water so essential for respiration. In the matter of maintaining life, when an animal has to choose between respiration and feeding, there is no doubt that it makes provision for respiration first.

One other important adaptation for life in the intertidal zone of a rocky shore is the ability to hold on to the rock surface, thereby preventing the animal from being swept away by the waves. The common saying, 'to

MARINE AND LAGOON ANIMALS—I

cling like a limpet' immediately comes to mind. The common limpet-like animal of our coasts is *Siphonaria grisea*, easily identified among

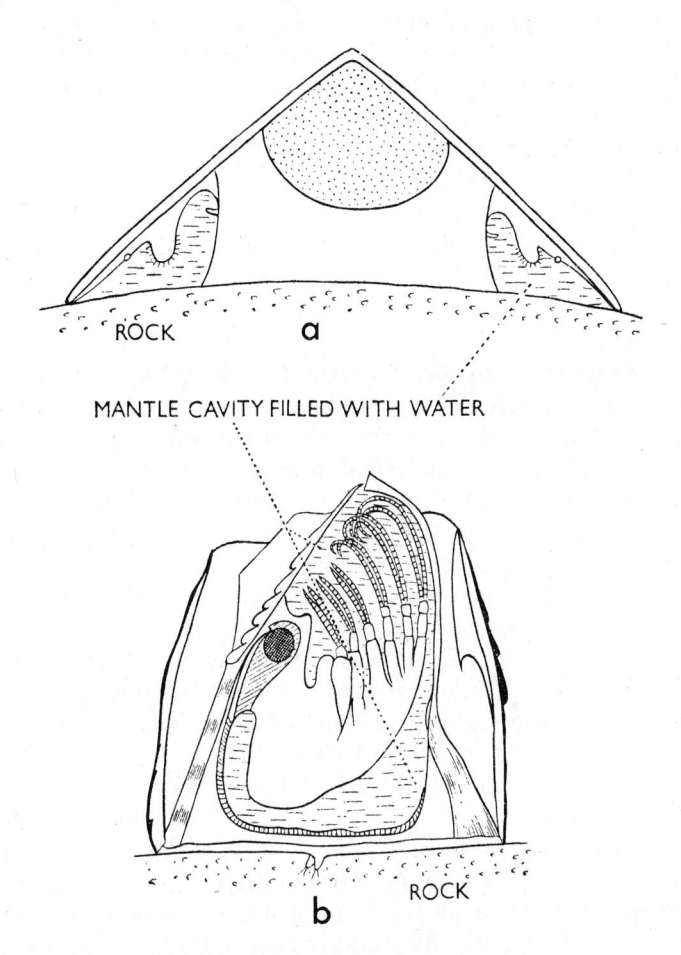

Fig. 26. Water retention during exposure by
(a) *Patella* (b) *Balanus*

other inhabitants by its conical shape. The shell of the 'limpet' is so well fitted to the rock surface on which it lies, and its foot holds on so firmly by suction, that considerable effort is required to dislodge it. The more one attempts to dislodge it, the firmer the foot holds. This is because each 'limpet' has a *home* which it has carefully created for itself by wearing down its shell to fit the contour of the rock at that spot. Although the animal moves about in search of food when covered by the water, it does not wander far, and will return to its home when the tide falls once more. The only other mollusc which may be mistaken for *Siphonaria* is the key-hole limpet *Fissurella nubecula*, but this has a hole at the apex of the conical shell, hence its common name.

The most abundant animals of the intertidal zone are the barnacles. Unlike limpets they are permanently cemented to the rock surface and even more effort (and a suitably shaped instrument) is required to dislodge them. Two common types easily identified on our coasts are the large *Balanus tintinabulum* found low in the intertidal zone, and the more common but much smaller *Chthamalus dentatus* which has a wider distribution within the zone.

Another group of animals of the intertidal zone which are adapted for holding on as securely as the limpets and barnacles are the **sea anemones**. These also occur low down in the intertidal zone where they are exposed for a short time. During this period, their tentacles are withdrawn and they maintain a near spherical shape. They may be found in large numbers on the sheltered sides of rocks, where they are not exposed to wave action. At the lowest level of the intertidal zone is the sea urchin *Arbacia lixula*, with its prominent long spines, and with its base firmly fixed to the rocks by the adhesive tube feet.

There are other animals in this zone which are not as firmly attached as the limpets, barnacles, sea anemones, and sea urchins already mentioned. These are usually to be found in the crevices and sheltered side of the rocks. A mollusc which may occur in large numbers is *Nerita senegalensis*. Its shell is black, but on close observation is found to have faint white stripes. There are also the carnivorous whelks *Thais haemostoma* which occur in large numbers, with their white egg capsules often forming a conspicuous matting on the rocks during their breeding season. These whelks are the largest molluscs in this zone and can easily be identified by the reddish colour of the opening of the shell.

Apart from the animals which are fixed or slow moving, a number of crabs of the genus *Plagusia* and fishes of the genus *Bathygobius* may be found. These are rather flattened and are thus adapted for moving easily into crevices. Furthermore they are both adapted for holding on to the rocks, the crab by the use of its claws and the fish by a modification of its pelvic fins to form a sucker. In intertidal rock pools are found the starfish *Asterina stellifera* and the 'sea mouse' (a shell-less mollusc) *Aplysia winneba*.

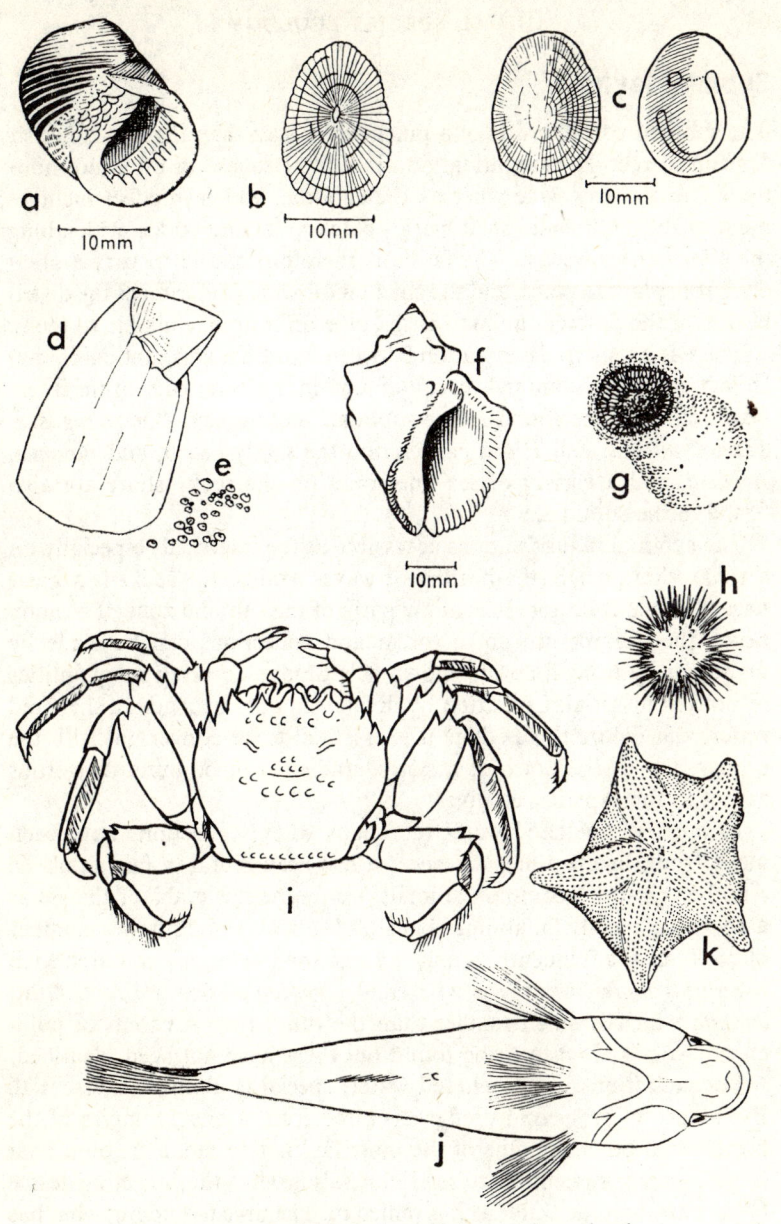

Fig. 27. Some animals of the intertidal zone of a rocky shore.

(a) *Nerita senegalensis*
(b) *Fissurela nubecula*
(c) *Siphonaria grisea*
(d) *Balanus tintinabulum*
(e) *Chthamalus dentatus*
(f) *Thais haemostoma*
(g) Sea anemone
(h) *Arbacia lixula*
(i) *Plagusia depressa*
(j) *Bathygobius sp.*
(k) *Asterina stellifera*

Subtidal fauna

The subtidal zone consists of a much wider area than the two zones so far considered. The supratidal and intertidal zones are often no more than a few metres wide whereas the subtidal, which in effect includes most of the continental shelf, varies between 23 and 60 km wide along the West African coast. The fauna is therefore bound to vary a great deal from place to place, and the chief factor which determines the distribution of the different animals is the type of bottom available to them.

There is no sharp demarcation between intertidal and subtidal fauna. In fact, most of the animals usually found in the lower edge of the intertidal zone are also found in the subtidal. *Astropecten*, *Donax rugosus*, *Terebra micans*, and *Hippa cubensis* on the sandy beach, and *Balanus*, *Arbacia*, and a variety of sea anemones on the rocky shore are also found in the subtidal.

The subtidal fauna is not as accessible as the intertidal, especially on a rocky shore where the beating of waves against the rocks is a great hazard to the collector. In shallow parts of the subtidal zone of a sandy beach the hazards are not as great and collections can be made by diving, or by using a device known as a dredge, to bring up quantities of bottom material. Collection by diving can only be made in sheltered water, and before this is done it is essential to be conversant with the topography of the bottom; a sharp gradient can be quite dangerous except to the experienced diver.

In areas of sheltered water off Lagos where collections have been made from time to time, *Astropecten* has been found in fair numbers. Another group of common animals are the hermit crabs of the genus *Clibanarius* mostly inhabiting shells of *Thais sp*. In addition a number of molluscs are frequently found: a large snail with grey coloured shell *Semifusus morio*, a large cowrie snail *Cypraea stercoraria*, and *Oliva anotata* which is much smaller than the other two. A variety of polychaete worms are also to be found but these have not been identified.

For collections in unsheltered water, special equipment is essential. By the use of grabs and dredge operated from a boat, samples of the bottom can be taken. One of the most fascinating moments on a boat (if you are not susceptible to sea sickness!) is when the collecting device breaks through the water as it is pulled in. The urge to find out what has been collected is overwhelming! A really modern method for the study of the subtidal fauna is an underwater closed television circuit. The cameras are let down into the water, and with appropriate lighting something of the life at the bottom can be shown on a screen. Even more modern devices are diving bells called **bathyspheres** and specialized submarines called **bathyscaphes** from which direct observations can be made. Finally, mention must be made of expert divers who are probably the most accurate investigators of the shallow subtidal fauna.

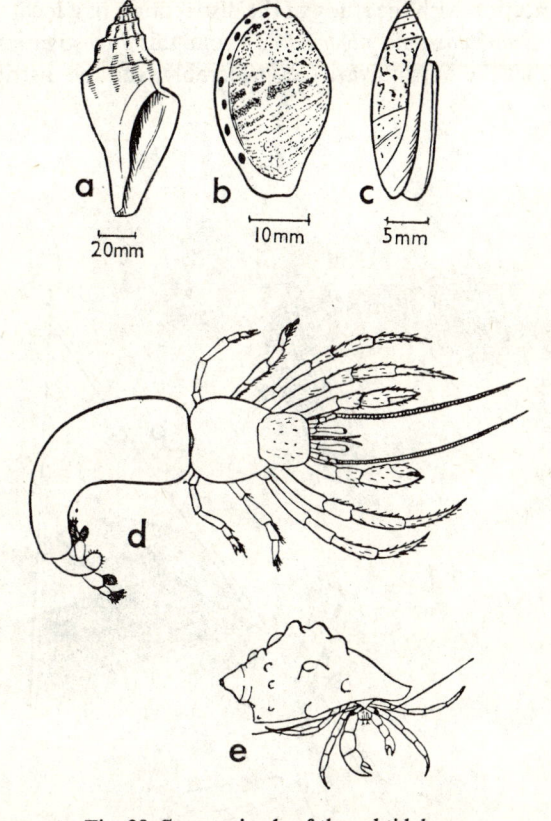

Fig. 28. Some animals of the subtidal zone.

(a) *Semifusus morio* (d) *Clibanarius africana* (out of shell)
(b) *Cypraea stercoraria* (e) *Clibanarius africana* (in shell of *Thais*)
(c) *Oliva anotata*

An area where the subtidal fauna has been carefully studied is off Accra in Ghana. From this work (Buchanan, 1958), it has been found that there are definite areas with different types of bottom, and each area has particular types of animals associated with it. In other words, there is some type of zonation. Between 0 and 4·5 metres, the familiar animals such as *Astropecten* and others of the intertidal zone were found to be widely distributed, but beyond this four clear zones were identified: (*a*) fine silt zone, (*b*) sandy silt zone, (*c*) silty sand zone, and (*d*) coarse sand zone.

The investigators clearly emphasized that each of the zones had a particular type of animal population associated with it.

A similar investigation of the subtidal zone off Lagos was made in 1955 in connection with the study of the distribution of a local species of amphioxus *Branchiostoma nigeriense*. From this investigation, it was discovered that the bottom varied considerably, and the distribution of

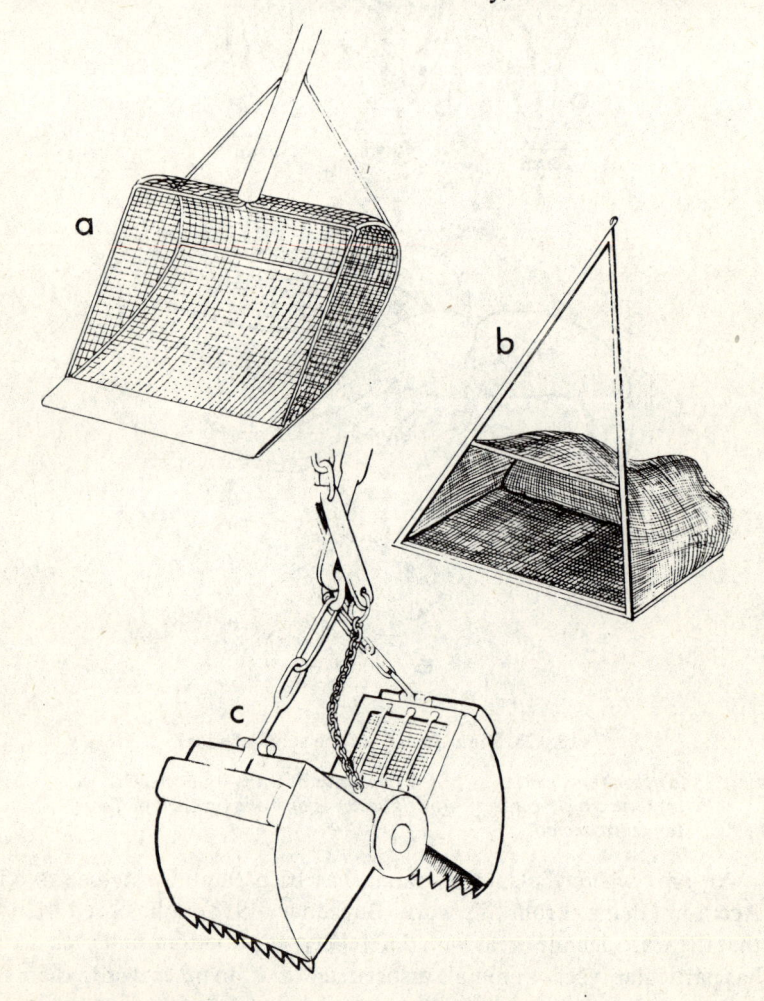

Fig. 29. Equipment for collecting bottom fauna.
(*a*) Scrapper net (*b*) Light dredge (*c*) Grab

MARINE AND LAGOON ANIMALS—I 67

the animal was patchy, occurring only where a suitable bottom was present.

Apart from amphioxus, other common sedentary animals are the heart urchin *Echinocardium sp.* and a variety of polychaetes and alcyonarians.

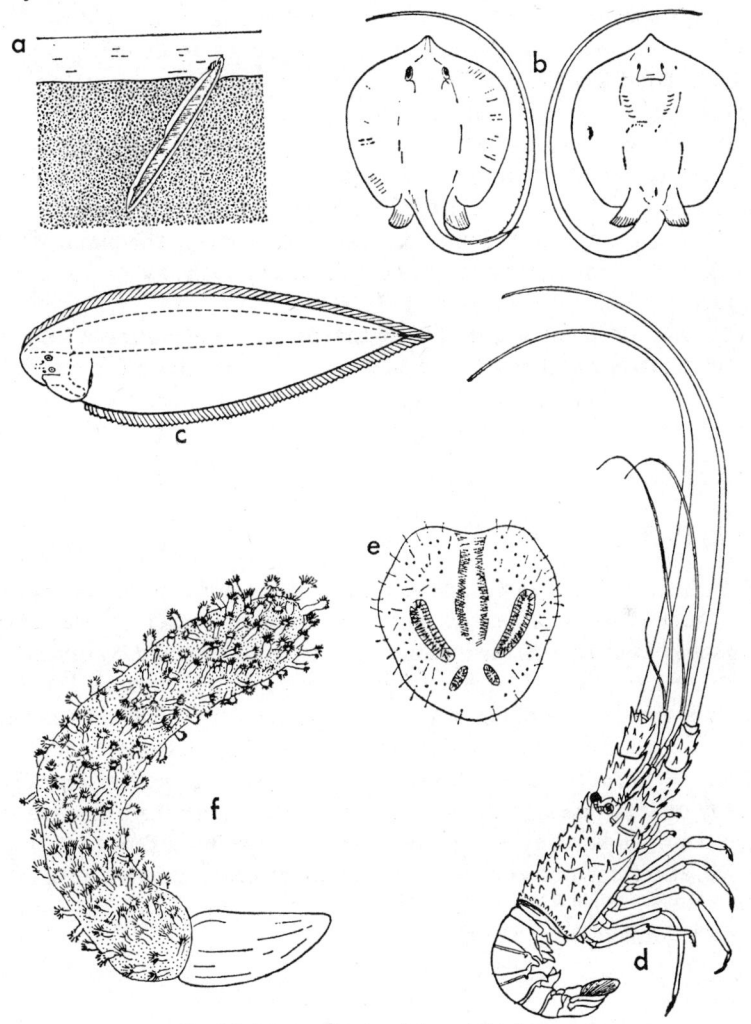

Fig. 30. More animals of the subtidal zone.
(a) *Branchiostoma nigeriense* (lancelet) (d) *Panulirus regius* (giant crawfish)
(b) *Trygon margarita* (sting ray) (e) *Echinocardium* sp. (heart urchin)
(c) *Cynoglossus lagoensis* (sole) (f) *Veretillum cynomorium* (Alcyonarian)

A trawl net usually catches fishes which live on the bottom or very close to it as well as the sedentary animals. Usually, their life is dependent on the sedentary animals of the bottom, as they feed mainly on molluscs. They may therefore be considered along with the subtidal fauna. Two well-known fishes, the sting ray *Trygon margarita* and the sole *Cynoglossus lagoensis*, are common and well adapted for life on the bottom. Although the former belongs to the group of cartilaginous fishes, chondrichthyes and the latter to the group of bony fishes Osteichthyes, they show similar adaptations, especially in their flattened form and mode of locomotion along the bottom. For most fishes locomotion is initiated by the lateral oscillation of a highly muscular but flexible tail. This is still true of the laterally compressed sole, but the sting ray has a greatly reduced tail and locomotion depends on the undulations of the greatly enlarged pectoral fins which make up the major part of its body.

Other animals found near the bottom are crawling crustacea such as crabs, crawfishes, and lobsters and among these, the giant crawfish *Panulirus regius* is worthy of mention as the largest crustacean found in our waters.

Shore birds

We must close our discussion of the marine littoral fauna by noting that there are a number of shore birds which depend on the other animals of this zone as their main source of food. The most conspicuous of these are so-called waders, a group of birds with longish legs for paddling in the edge of the waves, and long bills for probing the sand or mud for their prey. Common examples are the Common Sandpiper *Actitis hypoleucos* and the Whimbrel *Numenius phaeopus*. Incidentally, many of these waders are migrants that move to northern Europe to breed during our rainy season. Other birds like the Black Tern *Chlidonias nigra*, also a migrant, and abundant in the dry season at Lagos, dive into the shallow coastal waters to catch fish. These are shown with other aquatic birds in Figs. 52 and 53.

Lagoon fauna

In dealing with lagoon fauna, it is important to remember that we are considering life in brackish water in which there is variable fluctuation in abiotic factors with tide and seasons. Only a restricted number of species can exist under such conditions, and these few require particular adaptations to enable them to survive. It is inevitable that there must be some zonation in the distribution of lagoon fauna, varying from animals

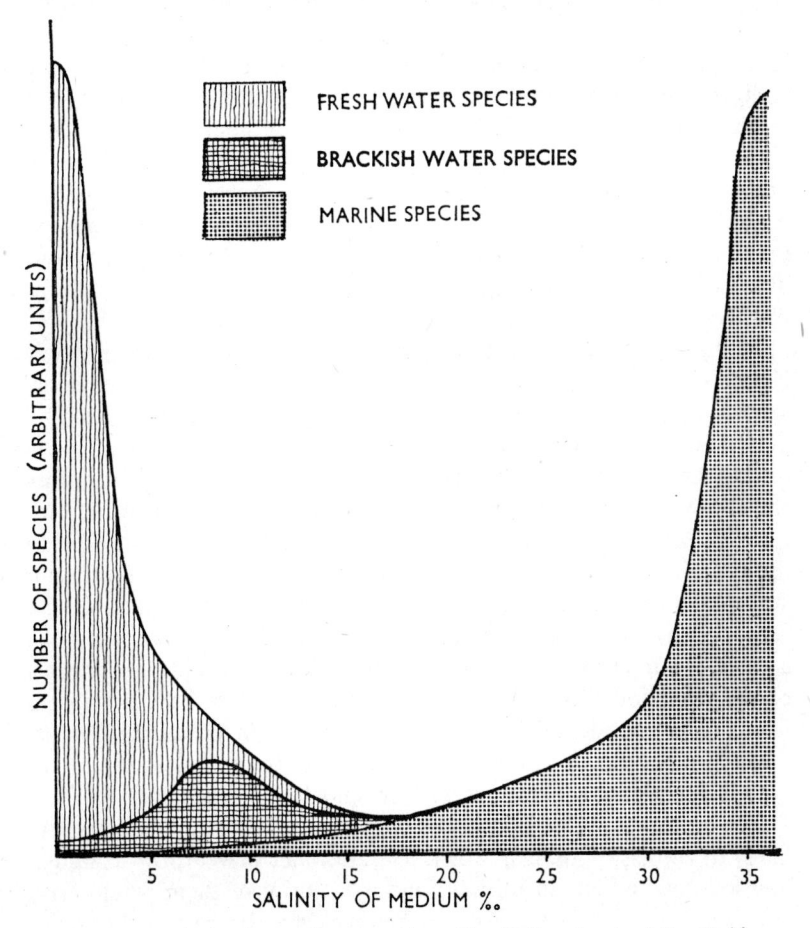

Fig. 30A. Variation in number of species with salinity of water (after Dahl, 1956).

with low salinity tolerance to those with high salinity tolerance in areas where change is greatest. In the first group are the marine animals which can tolerate a limited drop in salinity, and freshwater animals which can tolerate a limited rise in salinity. In the second group are the true brackish water animals with the necessary adaptations for life in brackish water. These are quite few. Fig. 30A shows the variation in the number of marine, brackish, and freshwater species with the salinity of the water.

The main adaptation for life in brackish water consists of regulating the concentration of the blood independently of the environment by some method of osmoregulation, or by having tissues which can tolerate large changes in the concentration of body fluids. The latter is the more common, and it would be interesting to make studies of our lagoon animals to find how they have adapted to life in brackish water. Three common European animals whose osmoregulatory mechanism in brackish water has been extensively studied are the common estuarine crab *Carcinus maenas*, the polychate *Nereis diversicolor*, and the common mussel *Mytilus edulis*. Animals similar to them are to be found in our brackish water, and nothing is known at present about their adaptations for life in brackish water.

In Fig. 31, a comparison is made of the salinity variation in four lagoon areas near Lagos in Nigeria. In (A) and (B), the seasonal fluctuation in salinity is great, for low tide in A, and for both low and high tides in B. The lowest low tide figure of approximately 0·5‰ in B during the rainy season, contrasts with 33·0‰ at high tide in A during the dry season to emphasize the extreme limits of seasonal variations. Area C, Kuramo waters, is also within the Lagos area but is joined to the main lagoon system by a narrow neck of water. It is therefore not susceptible to extreme salinity variation as are the other parts of the lagoon, variation being between 13·0‰ and 25·5‰. The area D, Ejinrin, is fairly stable, tending in fact to freshwater conditions for most of the year; and showing no tidal variation. Here we have four areas which differ considerably in terms of the variation in the salinity of water. The types of animals in the areas will depend on the possession of the type of functional adaptations which such situations require.

The bottom fauna of Ejinrin has not so far been studied, but it is very likely to consist of animals which tolerate water of very low salinities, and low fluctuations in salinity; and a majority of them would have migrated from freshwater. Area B, however, may be regarded as truly brackish with typical lagoon animals; typical in that they are to be found during most of the year.

The most common of these animals are the hermit crabs, previously mentioned as part of the marine fauna. In the lagoons, instead of inhabiting the shells of *Thais*, they inhabit the shells of two other snails, *Tympanostomus fuscatus* and *Pachymelania aurita*, which are common in the brackish water swamps. Hermit crabs are interesting crustacea.

They are closely related to the true crabs and have a similar type of development. After going through a number of larval stages they enter a suitable shell, making it their home. As they moult and increase in size, they select larger shells until they reach their adult size.

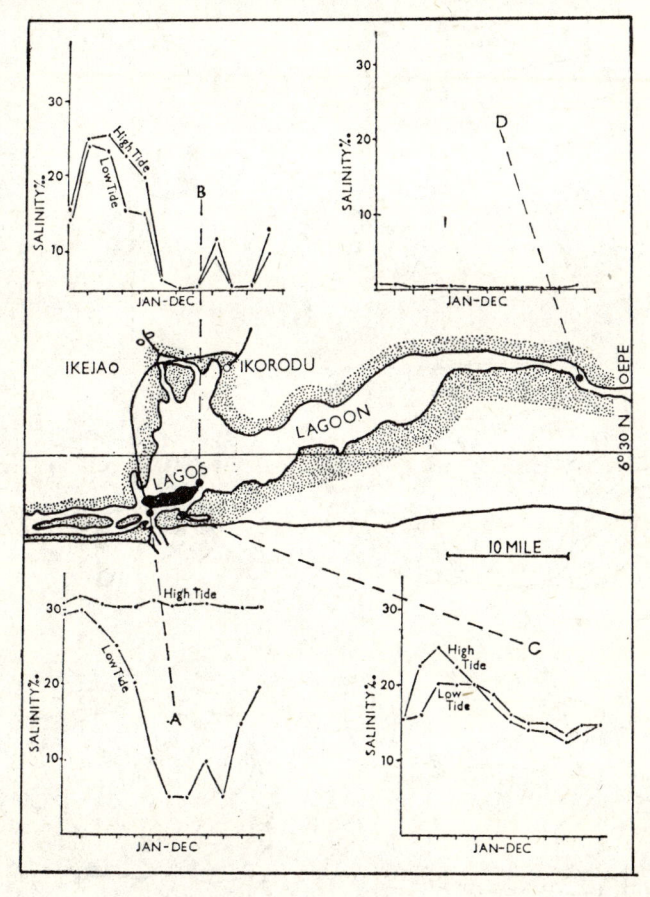

Fig. 31. Seasonal and tidal salinity variation in four lagoon areas.
- A. Lagos harbour
- B. Lagos lagoon
- C. Kuramo waters
- D. Ejinrin (56km east of Lagos)

They are well adapted for life in their shell, for one finds when one attempts to pull them out that they have specially modified legs for holding tightly to the shell. These legs are often broken before the animal can be pulled out.

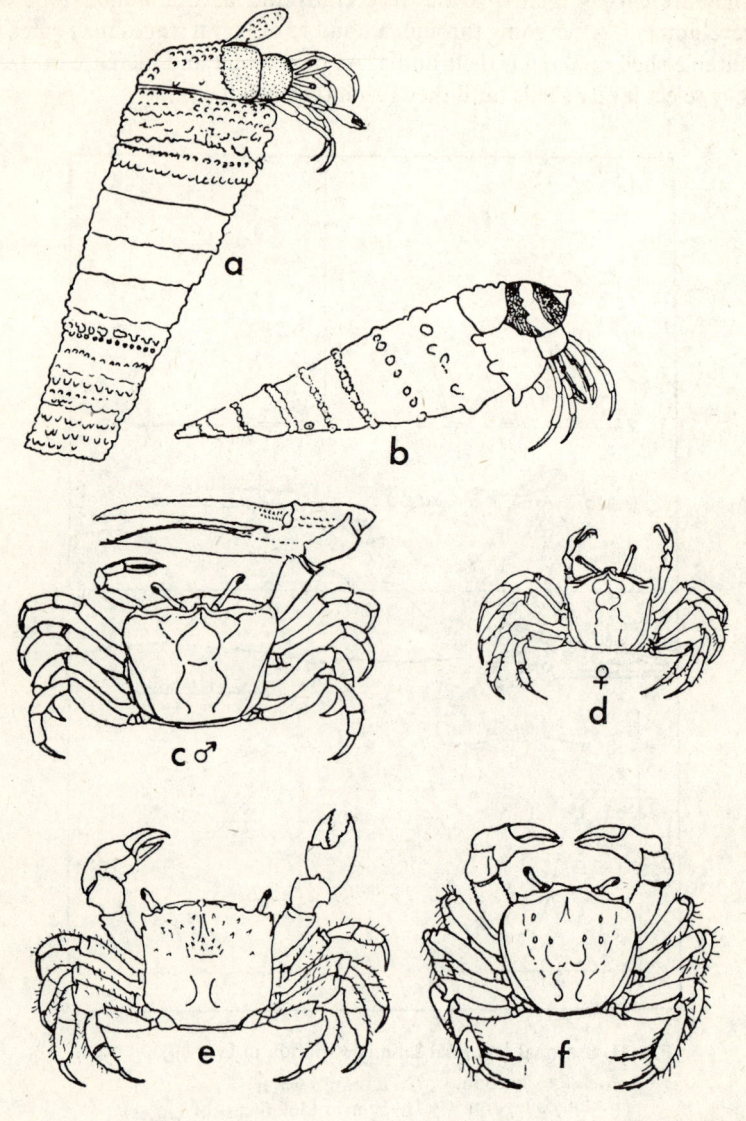

Fig. 32. Some

(a) Hermit crab *Clibanarius sp.* in shell of *Tympanostomus fuscatus*
(b) Hermit crab in shell of *Pachymelania aurita*
(c) *Uca tangeri* (male fiddler crab)
(d) *Uca tangeri* (female)
(e) *Sesarma huzardii* (hairy mangrove crab)
(f) *Cardisoma armatum* (common mangrove crab)

MARINE AND LAGOON ANIMALS—I 73

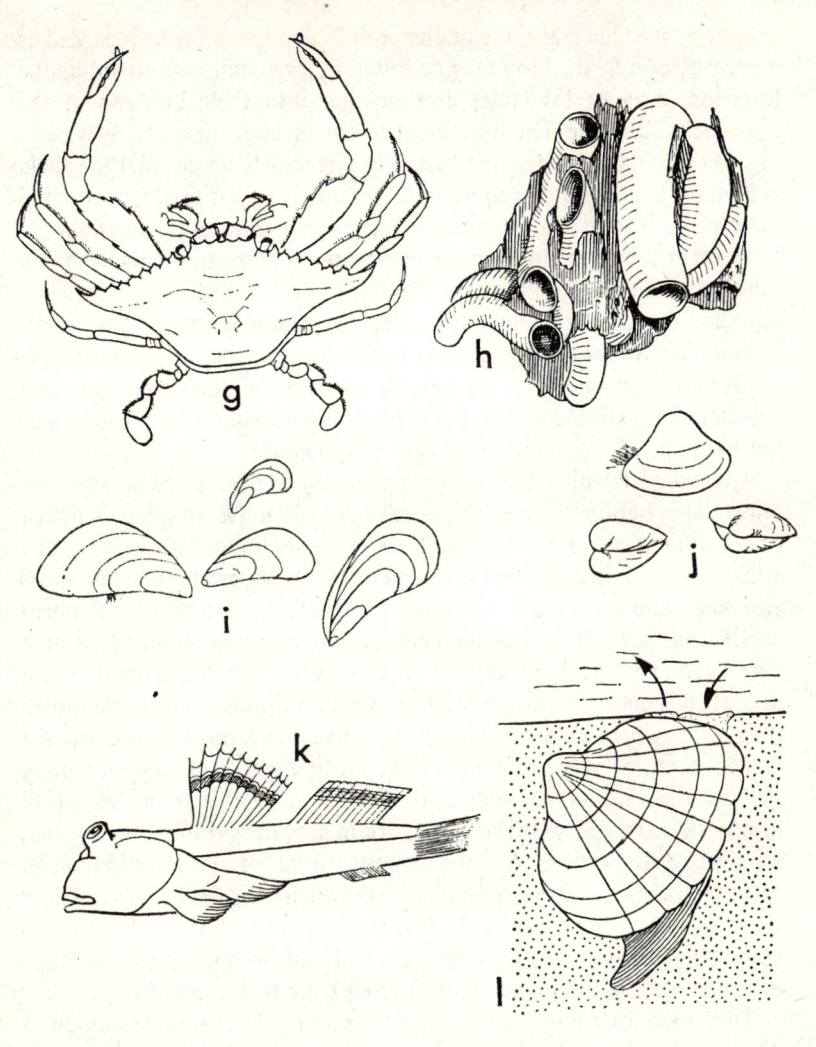

lagoon animals.

(g) *Callinectes latimanus* (swimming lagoon crab)
(h) *Bankia sp.* (*wood-boring mollusc*)
(i) *Brachyodontes niger*
(j) *Egeria paradoxa*
(k) *Periophthalmus koelreuteri* mudskipper)
(l) *Anadara* (*Arca*) *senilis* (bloody clam

Among the true crabs, the fiddler crab *Uca tangeri* may be regarded as a truly lagoon form. They may be found in large numbers crowding the intertidal area at low tide, disappearing into their burrows at the approach of danger. The movement of the chela of the male, as if playing a fiddle, earns it its common name. The male's single enlarged chela is used for defence and in courtship. The small chela is used for scooping sand grains into the mouth parts, while the first and second maxillipedes have stout setae for filtering organic material from the sand, which is rejected in the form of neat balls. Female hermit crabs have equal chelae and use both in feeding. Some other common lagoon crabs worth mentioning are the hairy mangrove crab *Sesarma huzardii*, found crowding round the roots of mangroves, the common lagoon crab *Cardisoma armatum*, often found wandering at night some distance from water, and the swimming lagoon crab *Callinectes latimanus*.

A lagoon fish which deserves special mention at this stage because it is intertidal in habit is the mudskipper *Periophthalmus koelreuteri*. This is a gobid which can swim normally like other fishes but can also carry out a variety of other movements such as **crutching, skipping,** and sometimes **climbing**. The movement described as crutching is a slow movement carried out with the aid of the pectoral fins in a way similar to a man using crutches. Such movement is common when the animal is not disturbed, hence it is not as well known as skipping, an escape movement with which most observers are conversant, and which earns the fish its common name. Here we have a fish capable of using a variety of land locomotory methods and which is also able to make use of atmospheric oxygen with the aid of certain accessory respiratory organs, admirable adaptations for the exposed mud of an intertidal area. *Periophthalmus* is a very specialized fish which suggests how the earliest land animals may have lived. The modification of its fins, although similar in function, are however very different in structure from those of the earliest land animals known from their fossil remains.

Two tube dwelling animals are common. The more common is *Mercierella enigmatica* found almost everywhere, but more especially on rhizophores of red mangrove, floating objects, and shells of other animals (see Plate I). They never show a sign of life when taken out of water, but if immersed again they soon push a beautiful whorl of tentacles from their tube. The second tube builder is a mollusc belonging to the genus *Bankia*; it is much larger than *Mercierella*, and groups of stout tubes, often intertwined to form a complicated mass, are found within old timber into which the animals have bored. In addition, there are often a variety of other annelids in the mud and sand.

Among the molluscs the gastropod *Littorina angulifera* and the bivalve *Gryphaea gasar* are commonly found on the roots of mangrove. Also common are a bivalve, *Brachyodonyes niger* which attaches itself to rocks and other surfaces, and on suitable sandy bottoms a small bivalve *Egeria paradoxa*.

One cannot state with any certainty that these animals are found throughout the lagoon system all the year round. This would only be possible if the animals are fully euryhaline, but there is at present no evidence that they are. Two of the few lagoon animals whose seasonal distribution, salinity tolerance, and life history have been studied in some detail are the local Nigerian lancelet *Branchiostoma nigeriense*, and the **bloody clam,** *Anadara* (Arca) *senilis*. The former is found in the lagoons around Lagos, where suitable sand is available, only during the period of high salinity; that is during the dry season. As soon as salinity falls to about 13‰ in June and July the lagoon populations perish. Before this takes place, however, the animals spawn between March and May and at ebb tide their larvae are swept out to sea where they may settle on suitable bottoms, thus replenishing the marine population. The marine population spawn in September and October, and at flood tide their larvae are then carried into the lagoons where they settle once again. Here then is an example of an animal known to be absent from the lagoons between May and November (a period of about half the year), but by a system of complementing each other, marine and lagoon populations are maintained. There is a high likelihood that this may apply to a large group of lagoon animals; but this can only be ascertained by studying the individual species concerned. From collecting records alone sea anemones, only found in the lagoons around Lagos in March and May, seem to have this pattern of distribution.

We now come to Kuramo waters, area C (see Fig. 31), in which the salinity fluctuation is less than in the more typical lagoon areas, being of the order of 12·0‰ between lowest and highest, as against 30‰ in the rest of the lagoon system. This difference is highly significant and probably accounts for the fact that a number of animals found in this area are not found elsewhere in the lagoon system. The best known of these animals is the bloody clam *Anadara senilis* already mentioned. It is significant that this animal is to be found only in this area of the Lagos lagoons, although it has a distribution in estuaries and lagoons along the whole of the West Africa Coast from Rio-de-Oro to Angola. It has been shown that this animal will not tolerate prolonged exposure to water of salinity below 6·5‰, and since this is the only part of the lagoon system where salinity does not normally fall below this limit, it is to be expected that the clam's distribution will be restricted in this way. Another mollusc which is also found here is *Semifusus morio*, already listed with the marine subtidal fauna. It is not commonly found in other parts of the lagoon system, presumably because it cannot tolerate a low salinity.

It is probable that there are other animals which, like *Anadara* and *Semifusus*, are confined to this area throughout the year. There may also be others which are confined to this area when salinity falls below tolerable limits in other parts of the lagoon, and repopulate the rest of the lagoon when salinity conditions are satisfactory in a way similar to that of the marine and lagoon populations of *Branchiostoma*. Prominent species of this area require to be investigated.

Bathyal and abyssal fauna

A consideration of the bottom marine fauna would be incomplete without some mention of the animals of the deep sea beyond the continental shelf. The groups of animals usually represented are molluscs, starfish, sea urchins, and various annelids.

The adaptations which enable these animals to withstand the great pressures which must obtain at these depths are still not understood. What is known is that they require to live under these high pressures since they fail to survive under less pressure when they are brought to the surface.

Two other common features of these animals deserve mention. Firstly, it is known that they are usually larger in size than related forms in the subtidal zone, so that so-called *'giant forms'* are found. Secondly they usually have a weaker skeleton, tending to be more fragile than their relations in the subtidal zone. This is partly due to the fact that calcium, which forms the greatest percentage of skeletal materials, is rarer in deep waters than in surface waters of the sea.

Things to do

A journey to the coast to study the bottom fauna described in this chapter is highly desirable. The following should be borne in mind when planning such a journey.

(i) *Time*. The best time is at spring tide, that is at new moon or full moon when you are likely to obtain the best tidal range, and the widest inter-

MARINE AND LAGOON ANIMALS—I

```
1 EHWS
2 MHWS
3 MHWN
4 LHWN
5 HLWN
6 MLWN
7 MLWS
8 ELWS
```

(a) High Gradient Beach

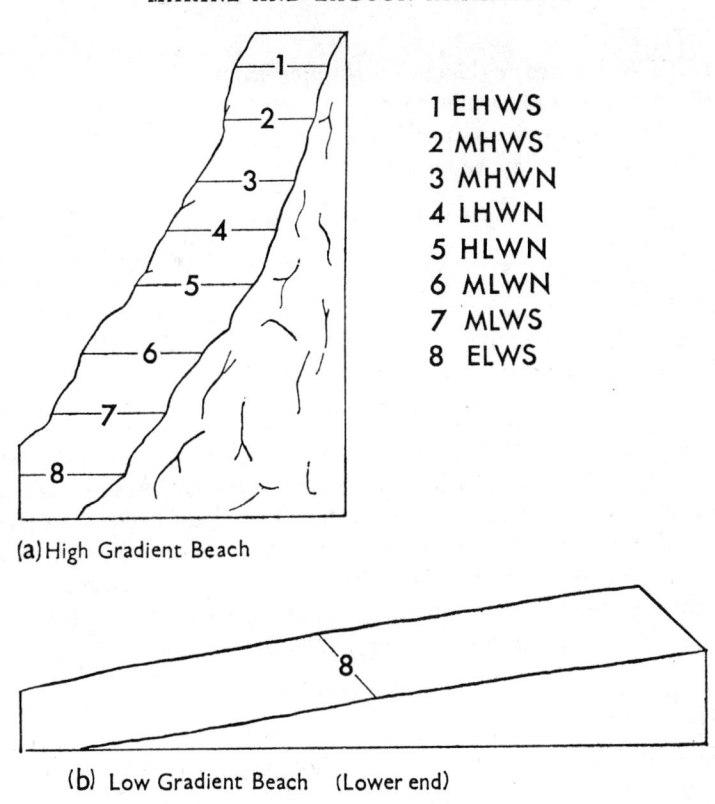

(b) Low Gradient Beach   (Lower end)

Fig. 33. High and low gradient beaches.

tidal zone will be exposed. The appropriate time for low tide may be obtained in advance from tables prepared by the Ports Authority of your area.

(ii) *Type of beach.* Both sandy and rocky beaches should be studied if available. The most suitable type on which to study zonation of the fauna is one in which the gradient of the slope is small, so that a wide area is exposed between tides even though tidal range may be small.

In studying the intertidal zone, the following tidal abbreviations and their meanings should be recognized in the following order.

EHWS Extreme high water springs
MHWS Mean high water springs
MHWN Mean high water neaps
E(L)HWN Extreme (lowest) high water neaps

MTL Mean Tide Level
E(H)LWN Extreme (highest) low water neaps
MLWN Mean low water neaps
MLWS Mean low water springs
ELWS Extreme low water springs

On a rocky beach, areas where water is left behind in shallow hollows, known as 'rock pools', are very useful because they usually sustain animals belonging to the subtidal zone. It is also convenient to observe the behaviour of these animals in such a pool. For example, sea anemones can be studied in this way, and their food preferences discovered by offering them a variety of molluscs found in the area, such as the littorinids, and *Donax* species. *Asterina* and *Aplysia* are also common.

(iii) *How to collect.* Collections should be systematic, and at the same time a record of the physical factors (such as temperature, salinity, wind, cloud cover, state of tide, etc.) should be made. Collections along selected transects or from a number of points within the same area (such as a square metre) are essential to be able to compare collections made at different times. Also note what animals are in breeding condition (e.g, female crabs carrying eggs, eggs attached to rock, etc.)

(iv) *Equipment.* The following are essential

Hand nets	
Scraper nets	
Spade	Sand collections
Sieve	
Rough forceps	
Scalpel or strong knife	Rock collections
Sample and specimen bottles	
4 – 5% formalin	Preserving collections
Metre rule or tape	
Centigrade thermometer	

(v) *Quantitative estimation.* Collections of a given species made from different areas, or at different times can be meaningfully compared only if a quantitative assessment is made, e.g. Count per unit area—or unit volume (m^2 and cm^3 are ideal).

(vi) *Zonation.* The term 'zonation' which has been used a number of times in this chapter requires some explanation. When we find that groups of animals and plants become adapted to particular zones within a given area, we say that there is zonation in that area. One of the best examples of zonation is found in the intertidal area, where some animals are restricted to the upper zone, some to the lower zone and others to the middle zone. It is rare to find an animal across the whole extent of the intertidal area. On a small scale the root of the Red Mangrove, shown in Plate Ib, shows zonation well. Within this small area we find an upper zone with a concentration of ***Chthamalus estuarii,*** and a lower zone with both ***Chthamalus*** and ***Balanus.*** In this case, ***Chthamalus*** is found all over but ***Balanus*** shows zonation.

It is to be borne in mind when making a study of or collecting specimens in the intertidal area that rocks, jetty, piling, or retaining wall, in the marine and brackish water often show zonation.

6: The marine and lagoon animals—pelagic forms

We now leave the bottom fauna of sea and lagoon to consider the animals which are found away from the bottom. The zones of open water based on the penetration of light, giving us the *photic* and *aphotic* zones, do not tally with the faunal divisions of open water, namely *plankton* and *nekton*. Plankton consists of drifting organisms whilst nekton are actively swimming animals. Although the bulk of plankton are found in the photic zone, the aphotic is not devoid of them. The nekton may be found near the surface, where they are described as *pelagic* down to the depths of the oceans, where they are described as *bathypelagic*.

The marine plankton

For convenience, the plankton is divisible into *zooplankton, phytoplankton* and *nannoplankton*. The first includes the animals, the second plants, and the third are such minute organisms as bacteria. (Plankton is a collective name, and the organisms are sometimes called *plankters*.)

A simple equipment for the collection of plankton is a *plankton net*. It is a conical net made of fine silk cloth into the end of which is inserted a metal or plastic container, which can be screwed on and off. As the net is pulled through the water, the water is filtered, and the plankton fished accumulates in the container at the end of the net. The size of plankters collected depends on the fineness or *mesh size* of the net. A net with a mesh size of about 70–80 meshes to a square centimetre is suitable for most collections. Although the mesh size of international nets varies from 7 to 80 per square centimetre, few of them are in common use as it is often adequate to use a fine net and a coarse net for most collections. When a boat is not available water may be filtered through the net simply by pumping or pouring it through. A hand net can also be used for small collections.

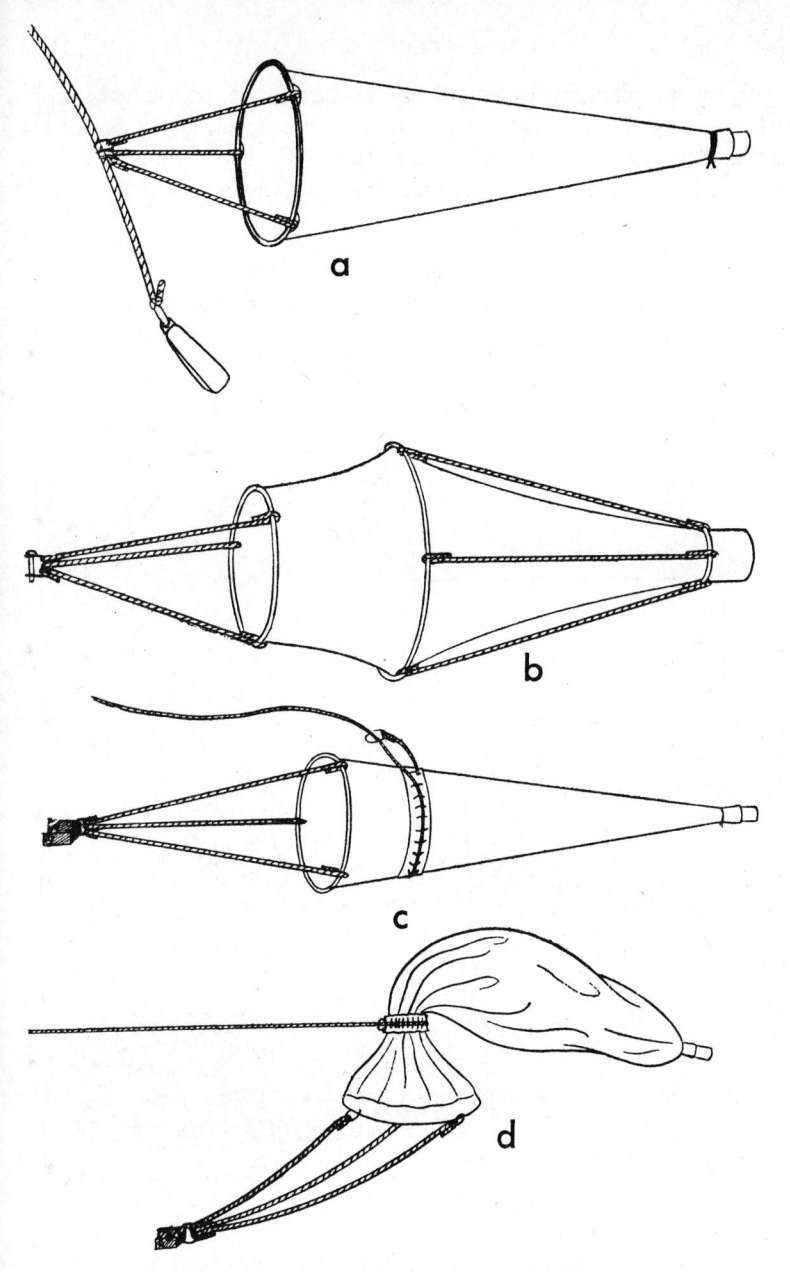

Fig. 34. Plankton nets (from Newell & Newell)
(a) Standard net
(b) Hensen net
(c) and (d) Net with closing device before and after closing

82   ANIMAL SPECIES ECOLOGY

When the plankton is poured into a glass bottle, one will see, even with the naked eye, or better still with a hand lens, that many organisms are present, moving vigorously in the water. However, it is only under a microscope that one can study planktonic organisms adequately.

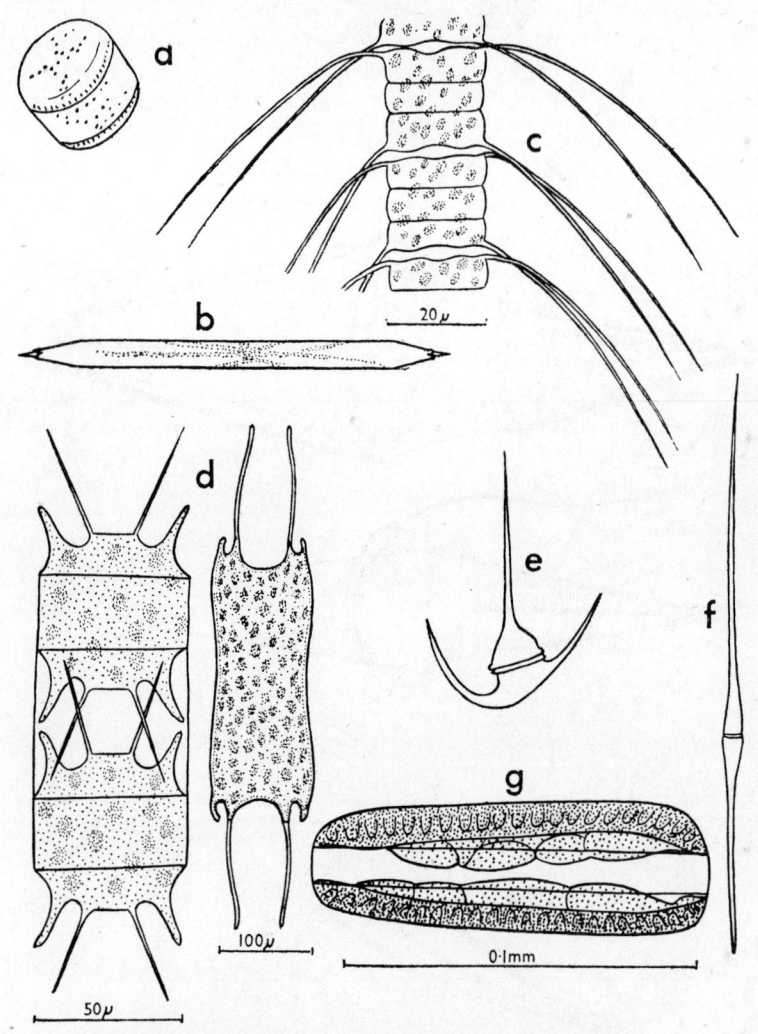

Fig. 35. Common marine and lagoon diatoms and dinoflagellates.
 (a) *Coscinodiscus sp.*
 (b) *Rhizosolenia sp.*
 (c) *Chaetoceros sp.*
 (d) *Biddulphia sp.*
 (e) *Ceratium tripos*
 (f) *Ceratium extensum*
 (g) *Surirella sp.*

It will be found that a small drop of the collection contains thousands of organisms, some with green colouring matter, and others without. In the study of plankton, it is usual to treat both phyto- and zooplankton together and, in spite of the fact that this is a study of fauna, this traditional approach will be adopted.

The phytoplankters, most of which are commonly known as *diatoms*, vary in form and size. They are unicellular, with a characteristic skeleton consisting of two valves, or *frustules* which overlap each other like two petri dishes of unequal size, to give a girdle also characteristic of diatoms. The skeleton consists of pectin and silica. Diatoms include disc shaped solitary forms such as *Coscinodiscus*, spindle-shaped forms such as *Rhizosolenia*, and chained forms such as *Biddulphia* and *Chaetoceros*. Some phytoplankters are capable of locomotion by the use of a pair of flagellae, one in a transverse groove and the other trailing along the main axis of the cell. These are called *dinoflagellates.* Some, like *Noctiluca*, although they can photosynthesize food, are holozoic whilst others are saprozoic. Two species of *Ceratium*, *C. tripos* and *C. extensum*, are common dinoflagellates in our waters.

Although these organisms are minute (a relatively large specie of *Coscinodiscus* is about 250 μ or $\frac{1}{4}$ mm in diameter), they occur in such large numbers, sometimes up to millions per litre of water during the peak season, that they colour the water a deep green. They are the primary producers of food upon which all the animals of the sea ultimately depend.

The zooplankton consists of two main groups of animals. First, there are the larvae of other organisms which are only planktonic during the larval phase but become nektonic or benthonic in adult life. These form the **temporary zooplankton.** Other zooplankters which remain planktonic throughout life form the **permanent zooplankton.**

Some common planktonic larvae are shown in Fig. 36. Of these, the nauplius larvae of barnacles are the most abundant, being found in the plankton during most of the year. They are easy to identify, their triangular shape showing up among all the other animals, which generally tend to be circular or elongated. Although the other larvae are not as plentiful, their occurrence immediately reminds one of the common animals listed for the bottom marine fauna in Chapter 5.

By far the most abundant of the permanent zooplankton are the copepods. They are to a marine habitat what insects are to a land habitat. Like diatoms, they may sometimes occur in such large numbers that they colour the water brown or red depending on the dominant species. Different species reach their peak at different times of the year,

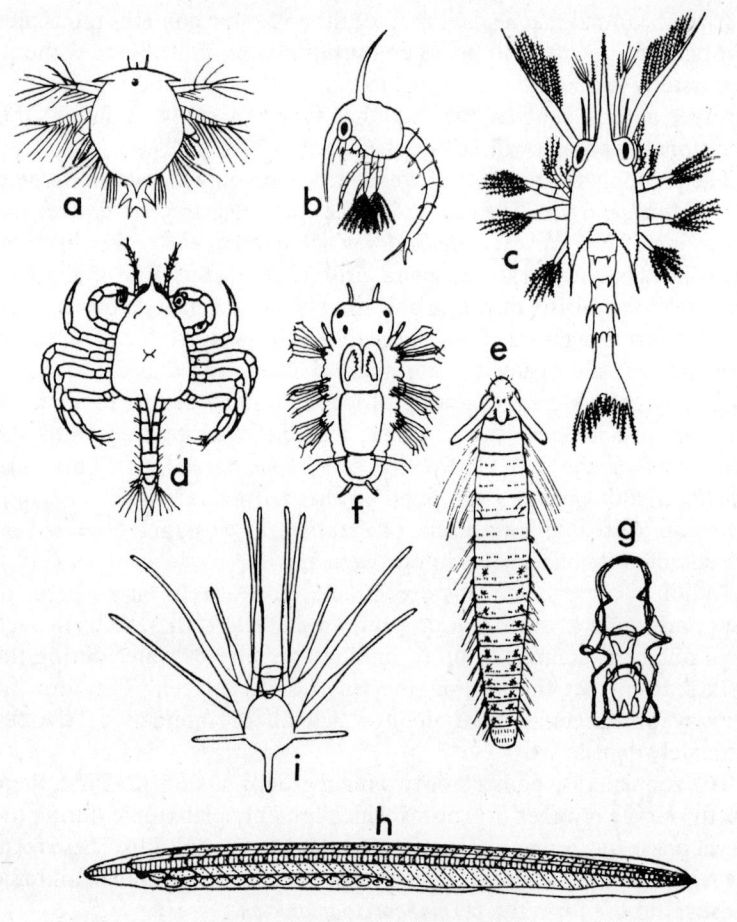

Fig. 36. Temporary zooplankton.

(a) *Nauplius* larva of *Chthamalus*
(b) *Zoea* larva of crab
(c) *Zoea* larva of hermit crab
(d) *Megalopa* larva of crab
(e) *Spionid* larva of polychaete worm
(f) *Nereid* larva
(g) *Pluteus* larva of *Astropecten*
(h) Larva of *Branchiostoma nigeriense*
(i) *Echinopluteus* larva of sea urchin

but by far the commonest copepods in our marine waters are two species of *Paracalanus*, *P. parvus* and *P. pygmaeus*, and also *Acartia clausii*. Other copepods commonly found, and shown in Fig. 37, include *Temora turbinata, Euterpina acutifrons, Centropages furcatus, Oithona nana, Corycaeus obtusus, Oncaea venusta, Candacia pachydactyla, Rhincalanus nasutus,* and *Sapphirina nigromaculata*. These copepods you will find can

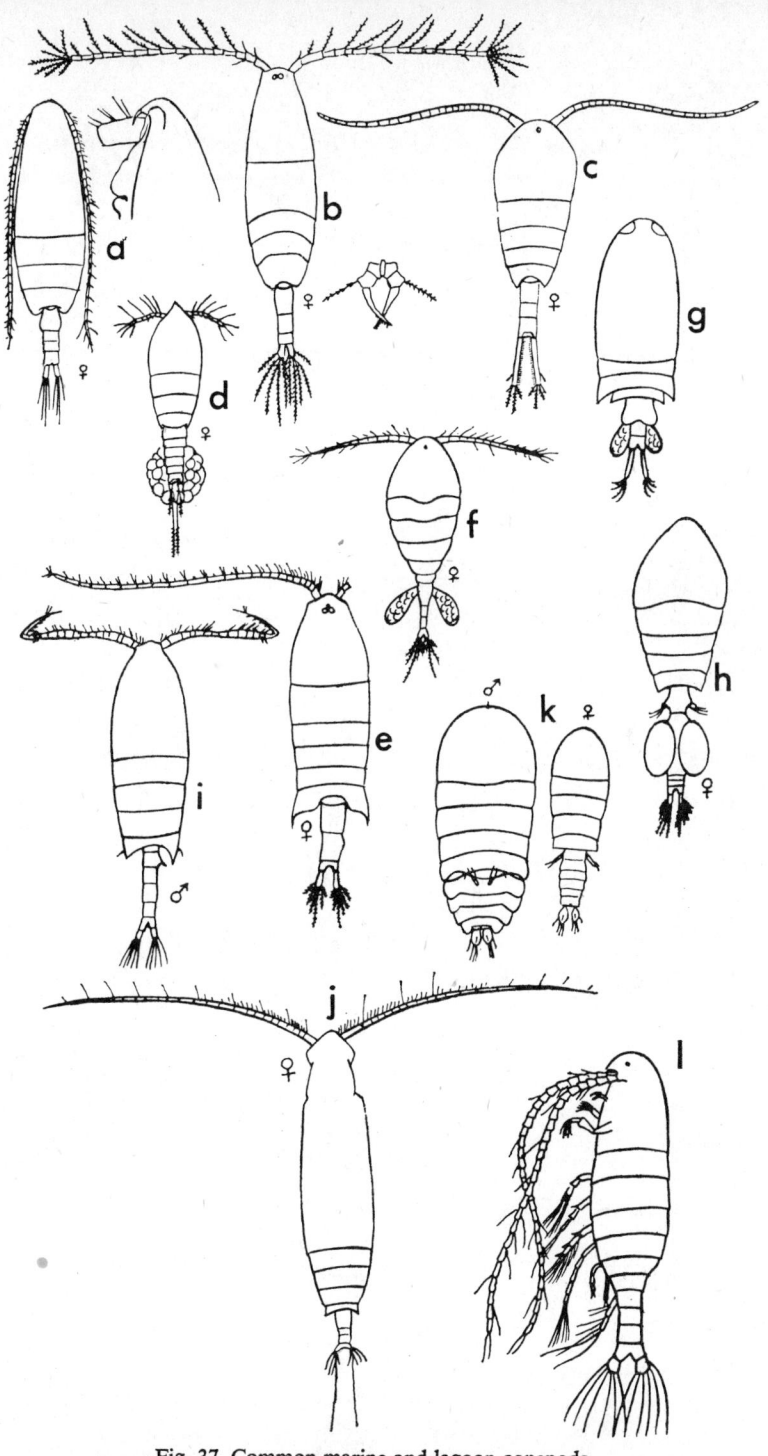

Fig. 37. Common marine and lagoon copepods.

(a) *Paracalanus pygmaeus* (b) *Acartia clausii* (c) *Temora turbinata*
(d) *Enterpina acutifrons* (e) *Centropages furcatus* (f) *Oithona nana*
(g) *Corycaeus obtusus* (h) *Oncaea venusta* (i) *Candacia pachydactyla*
(j) *Rhincalanus nasutus* (k) *Sapphirina nigromaculata* (l) *Diaptomus sp.*

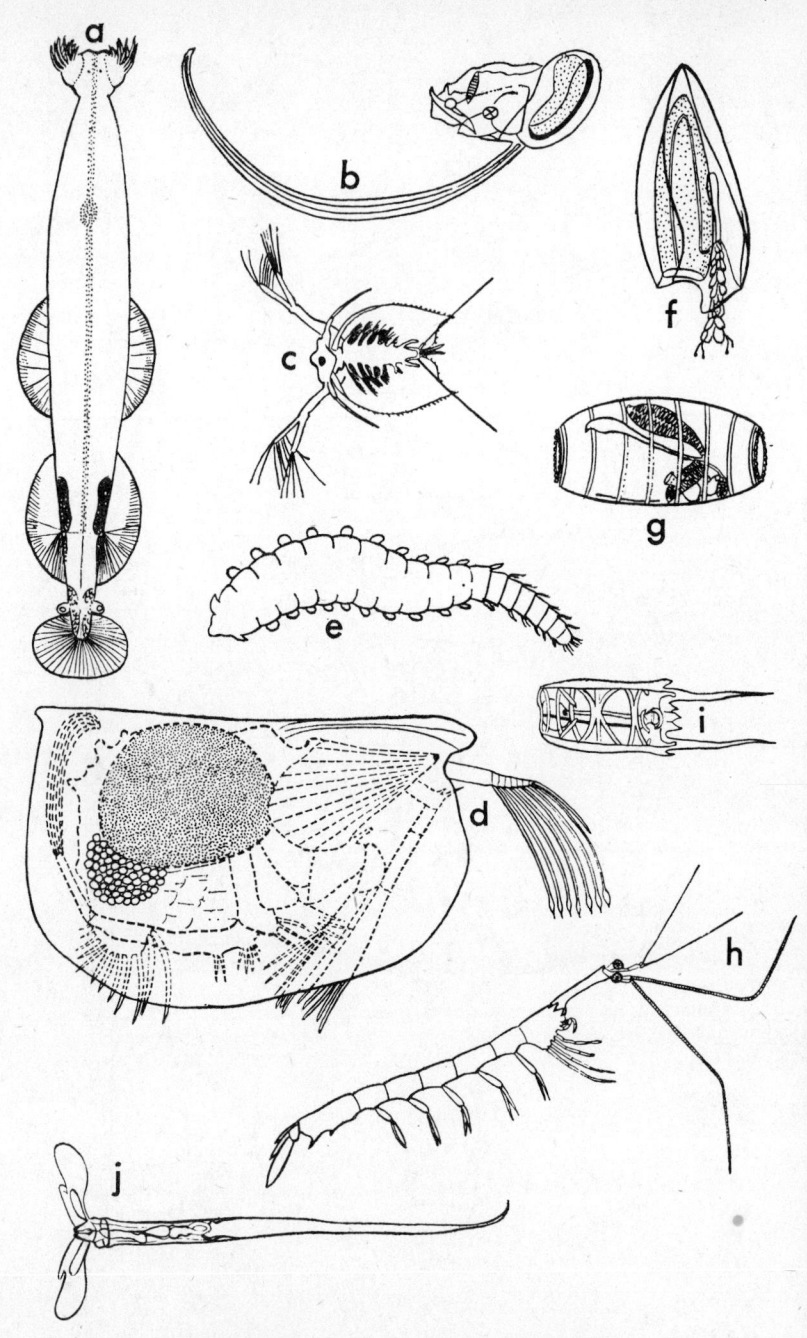

Fig. 38. More marine permanent zooplankton.

(a) *Sagitta enflata*
(b) *Oikopleura longicauda*
(c) *Penilia avirostris*
(d) *Conchoecia sp.*
(e) *Typhloscolex mulleri*
(f) *Muggiaea kochii*
(g) *Dollioleta gegenbauri*
(h) *Lucifer foxonii*
(i) *Salpa democratica*
(j) *Creseis acicula*

MARINE AND LAGOON ANIMALS—II

tolerate some variation in salinity so that collections in brackish water, especially at high tide, usually include some of them.

Apart from copepods, most other phyla of animals are represented in the permanent zooplankton although in more modest numbers. *Sagitta*, the **arrow worm** (so called because it darts like an arrow), is quite common and is easily seen even with the naked eye. The two common species, *Sagitta friderici* and *Sagitta enflata*, tolerate submarine salinity. The larvacea, *Oikopleura longicauda*, is also of a size easily seen with the naked eye.

Planktonic organisms have certain characteristics in common. The most important is their ability to float in water. To be able to do this, the specific gravity of the animal must be the same or less than that of the surrounding medium. The development of an air filled float is one method adopted by *Physalia*, the **Portuguese man of war,** which has a large one, but not by any of the animals mentioned so far. It has been recorded on the coast off Accra in Ghana and from Lagos in Nigeria and although it is an oceanic form it may sometimes be washed ashore. A more common method is by increasing the surface area of the body, by the development of spines and other similar structures.

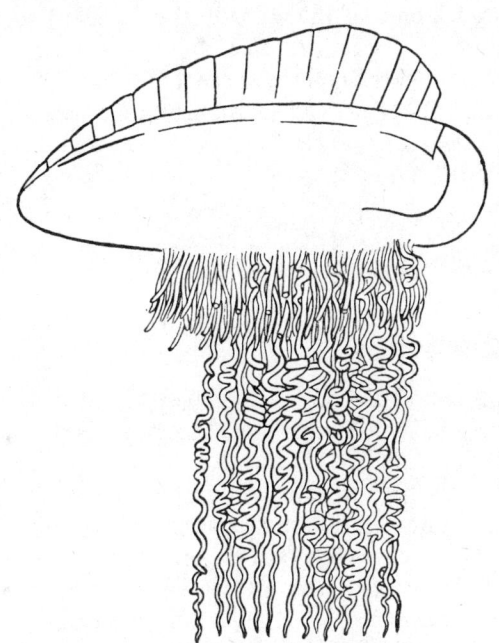

Fig. 39. *Physalia*, Portuguese man of war.

If you look at Figs. 35–38 again, you will notice that many of the organisms are equipped with spines of various sorts. The effect of increasing the surface area is to increase the *frictional* resistance of the body. Now, this requires some explanation and to help in this, I would ask you to cast your mind back, and see yourself as a small boy or girl, washing your writing-slate in a stream or a large basin of water. If you placed your slate edgeways it sank quickly but if placed flat, it sank slowly. The explanation for this is that a wider surface is associated with the water surface when the slate is placed flatways, leading to greater frictional resistance. The greater the surface area in relation to weight, the more difficult it is to sink, and by increasing surface area it is possible to reach a situation in which the frictional resistance counterbalances the gravitational force and the organism remains afloat.

Lagoon plankton

What has been said about marine plankton applies in general to lagoon plankton also. The main difference is that the organisms of the lagoon system are those which are able to tolerate more variable and submarine salinities. Some of the animals already listed for the sea are found in the lagoon system and chief among these are the copepods, *Acartia clausii* and *Oithona sp.* which seem to be able to tolerate a wide range of salinity. Other permanent zooplankton include various other *copepods*, *cladocera*, *rotifers*, *molluscs*, and *arachnids*, typical of brackish water, and among the larvae, those of the barnacle and crab are the most common.

Phytoplankton consists mainly of species of *Chaetoceros*, *Biddulphia*, and *Surrirella*. A variety of algae, including *Volvox*, are also found.

Plankton distribution

The distribution of plankton is usually uneven. This, of course, is what would be expected considering the fact that planktonic organisms are carried by currents and do not depend on their own locomotory ability to direct themselves. Even within the same body of water it is often found that although the same species are present at a particular time, the density of population varies considerably from one part to another. Local differences in density of this sort are difficult to investigate because sometimes they may be attributable to collection methods; nevertheless, the uneven distribution of plankton is universally recognized.

Seasonal variation in plankton distribution is another point of

Year/Month	Shark	Ray	Sea catfish	Threadfin	Bigeye	Croaker	Moonfish	Miscl.
1960 January	11·6	31·7	63·7	38·5	45·4	87·9	3·7	55·8
February	11·7	27·0	61·7	32·7	36·7	62·4	6·8	50·7
March	12·0	19·5	44·1	57·1	39·4	80·4	9·6	47·7
April	7·6	20·8	40·0	32·0	28·4	61·3	5·6	63·1
May	6·5	36·3	37·5	56·3	28·0	64·0	5·5	93·4
June	5·2	18·1	27·3	23·8	17·7	42·8	4·6	61·6
July	6·7	14·5	24·8	25·9	17·8	62·3	4·6	70·6
August	7·1	16·8	35·0	30·0	27·1	100·7	5·2	67·3
September	3·7	9·6	28·8	16·4	25·8	86·5	4·5	43·9
October	2·8	7·3	25·7	16·1	12·0	66·4	3·9	54·1
November	5·0	10·1	28·7	28·2	14·2	103·2	3·9	84·5
December	8·4	11·1	37·0	32·7	20·6	72·4	5·8	78·2
Total	88·3	222·8	454·3	389·7	313·1	890·3	63·7	770·9

Table IV. Landings (in metric tons) of major species of fish by trawlers in Lagos, 1960 (from Federal Fisheries Report).

90　　　　　　ANIMAL SPECIES ECOLOGY

interest. Even with rough and ready methods, it is not difficult to note seasonal changes of various organisms. Collections should be made regularly with the same type of net, fishing as far as possible over a

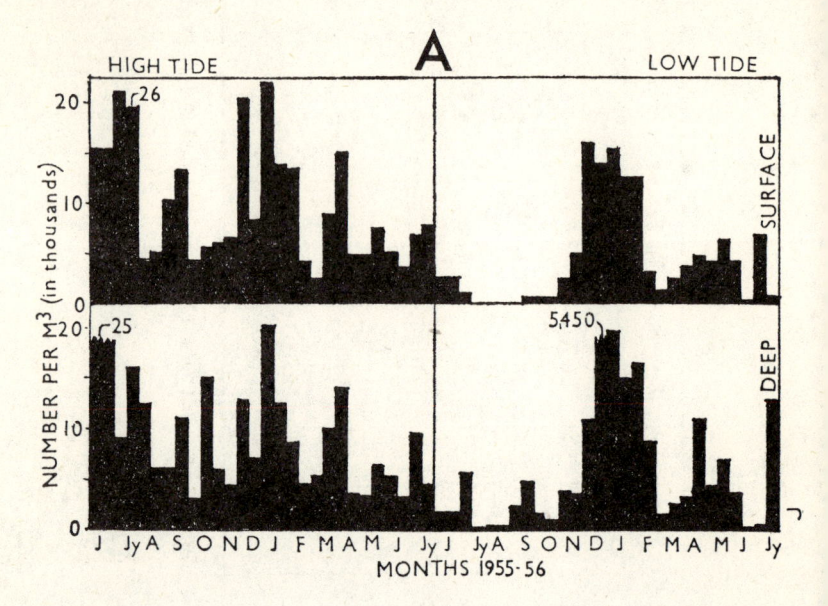

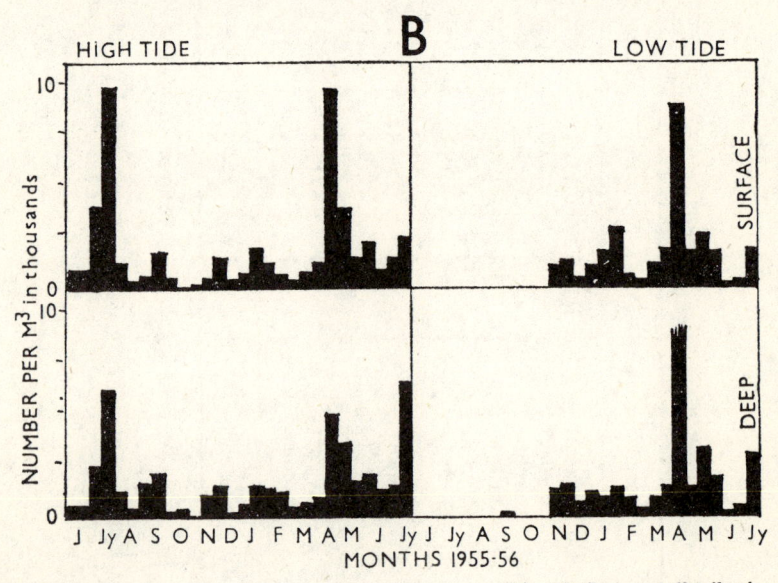

Fig. 40. Seasonal distribution
A. *Pseudodiaptomus* sp.
B. *Euterpina acutifrons*

given distance or for the same length of time. In this way, the total amount of plankton and the variation in abundance of individual species can be studied. Results from these types of studies carried out in

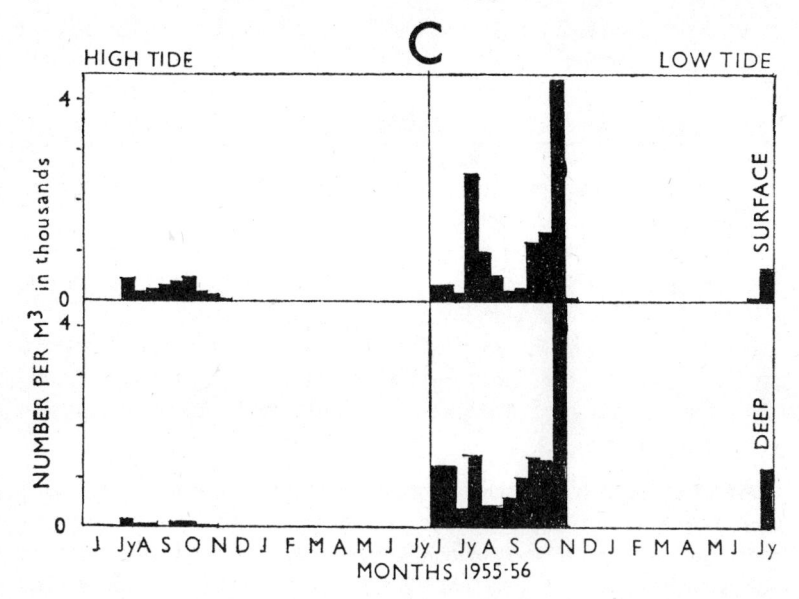

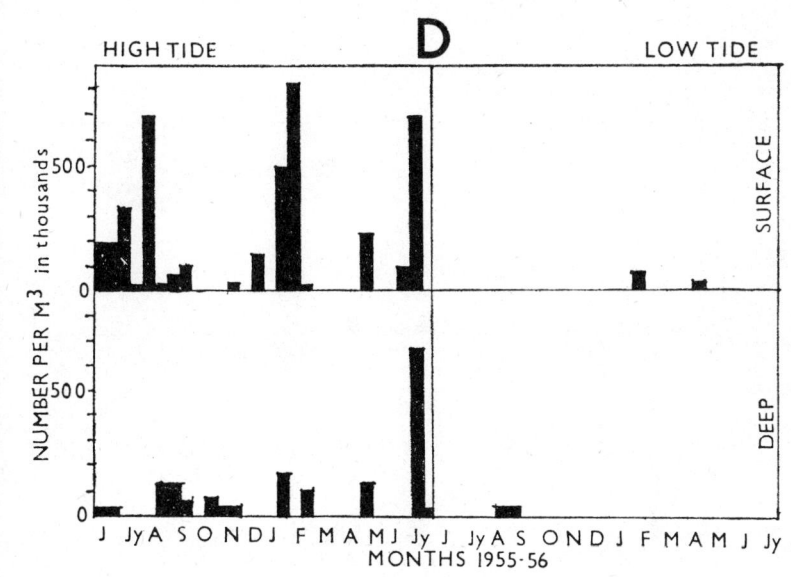

of some planktonic animals.

C. *Bosmina longirostris*
D. *Oncaea venusta*

the Lagos harbour and lagoon system show that the chief factor which influences seasonal distribution is the salinity of the water, the animals falling into four groups depending on their salinity tolerance.

(a) **Fully Euryhaline** are found in the harbour most of the year at high and low tide and in the lagoon system. These have the widest range of salinity tolerance, and such species are few in number.

(b) **Brackish (high salinity)** animals which tolerate salinities as low as 20‰ and are found in the harbour only at high and low tide during the high salinity season, but absent during the rainy season when salinity falls below 20‰.

(c) **Brackish (low salinity)** which will tolerate only low salinities, occurring at high and low tides during the low salinity season and absent during high salinity.

(d) **Neritic Stenohaline forms** show virtually no tolerance of lowered salinity and are only found in the harbour at high tide during the high salinity season when conditions in the harbour are essentially marine.

Another interesting aspect of plankton distribution is the variation with depth. There are some organisms which tend to remain permanently away from the surface but there are others which show an active vertical migration so that their density of occurrence depends on the time of day. A good example of the first group are the mysids, and Fig. 41 shows the results of collections made in 1955 and 1956 in the

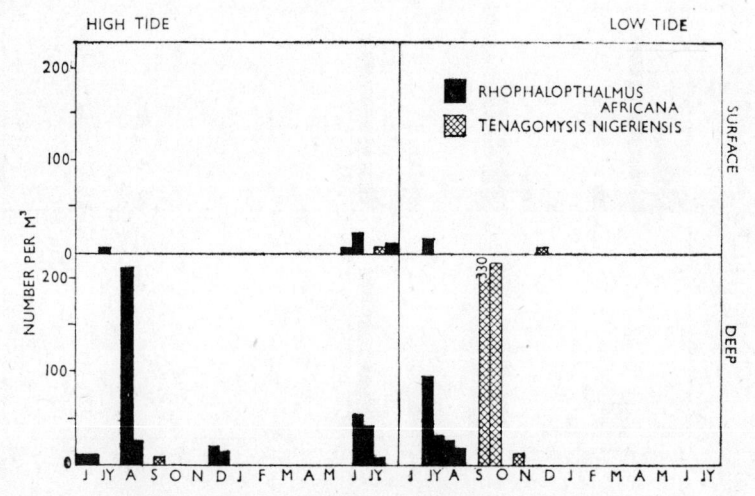

Fig. 41. Distribution of mysids in Lagos area 1955–56.

Plate III. Throwing a cast net on Lagos lagoon

(a)

Plate IV. Breeding behaviour of *Tilapia heudeloti*
    (a) Female laying eggs
    (b) Male fertilizing eggs
    (c) Male sucking eggs into mouth

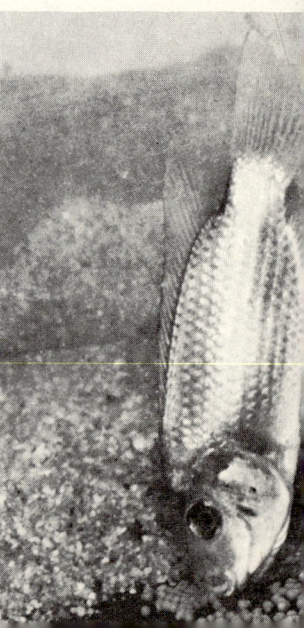

(b)

Plate V. Breeding behaviour of *Tilapia heudeloti* (cont'd)
(d) All eggs picked up by male
(e) Operation completed (note egg showing in mouth)

Plate VI. Giant termitarium of *Macrotermes* near Jebba, Nigeria

Lagos area. The results of these collections, made every 2 weeks in surface water and at a depth of 8 metres, show clearly the distribution of the two common mysids, *Tenagomysis nigeriensis* and *Rhophalopthalmus africana*.

Although planktonic organisms are not capable of vigorous locomotory movements, yet they are able to migrate from the surface to deep waters and *vice versa*. It has been found that the copepod *Calanus finmarchicus* of temperate waters, which has been studied a great deal, can migrate as much as 60 metres to bottom waters and back again every 24 hours. It is now generally known that plankton is more abundant in surface waters at night than during the day. Various explanations of this **diurnal rhythm,** based on a variety of factors, have been put forward by different authors; but so far there has been no entirely satisfactory explanation, and such details are outside the scope of this book. It is interesting to note however, that certain copepods of the genus *Corycaeous* (see Fig. 37(g)) carry out a reverse movement, coming to surface waters during the day and moving to bottom waters at night. It is important that any explanation of vertical migration should not exclude this type of migration.

The marine nekton

Nektonic animals, like those of the subtidal zone, are beyond the reach of the average collector, except one who is lucky enough to possess a boat and fishing gear. The most commonly used type of fishing net is the **cast net,** which is found in most fishing villages in West Africa. Other methods used range from hooks and bait to various types of traps and nets. Modern marine fishing requires the use of larger and more efficient nets. There are two main types, the **seine net** for fishing in surface waters and the **trawl net** for catching demersal forms. The former can be operated from a boat or from a base on the ground, the principle being to enclose an area of water by circling it with the net and gradually enclosing the animals within the area. The types of animals collected will depend on the mesh size; the finer the mesh, the more varied in size the animals will be. The trawl net is similar in principle to a plankton net, and is pulled along by a boat collecting animals along its course. Most nets are designed for trapping fish so that the bulk of nektonic organisms caught consists of them. However, a few other animals such as the swimming crab, *Callinectes gladiator*, the squid *Loligo*, and various prawns and shrimps are often caught in our waters.

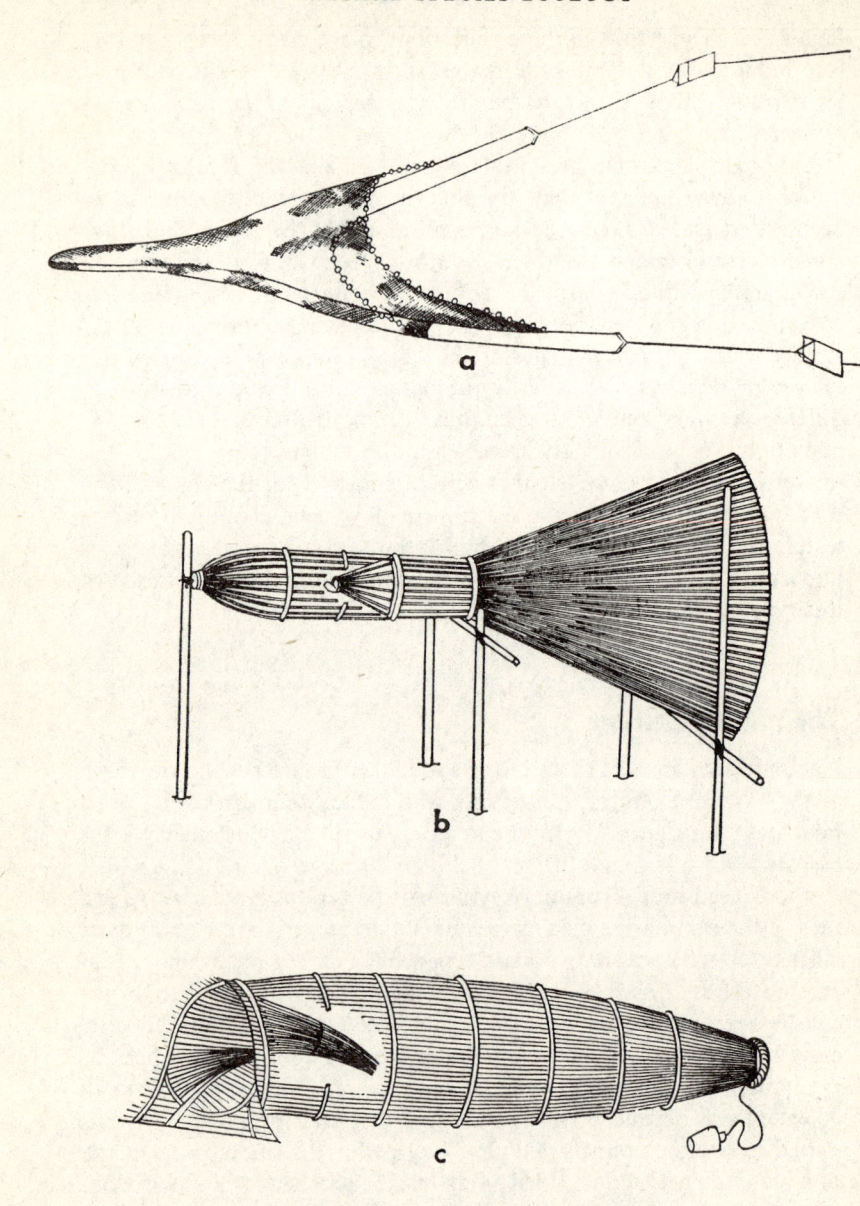

Fig. 42. Types of fishing nets and traps.
(a) Trawl net   (b) and (c) Fishing traps
(See also Plates II and III.)

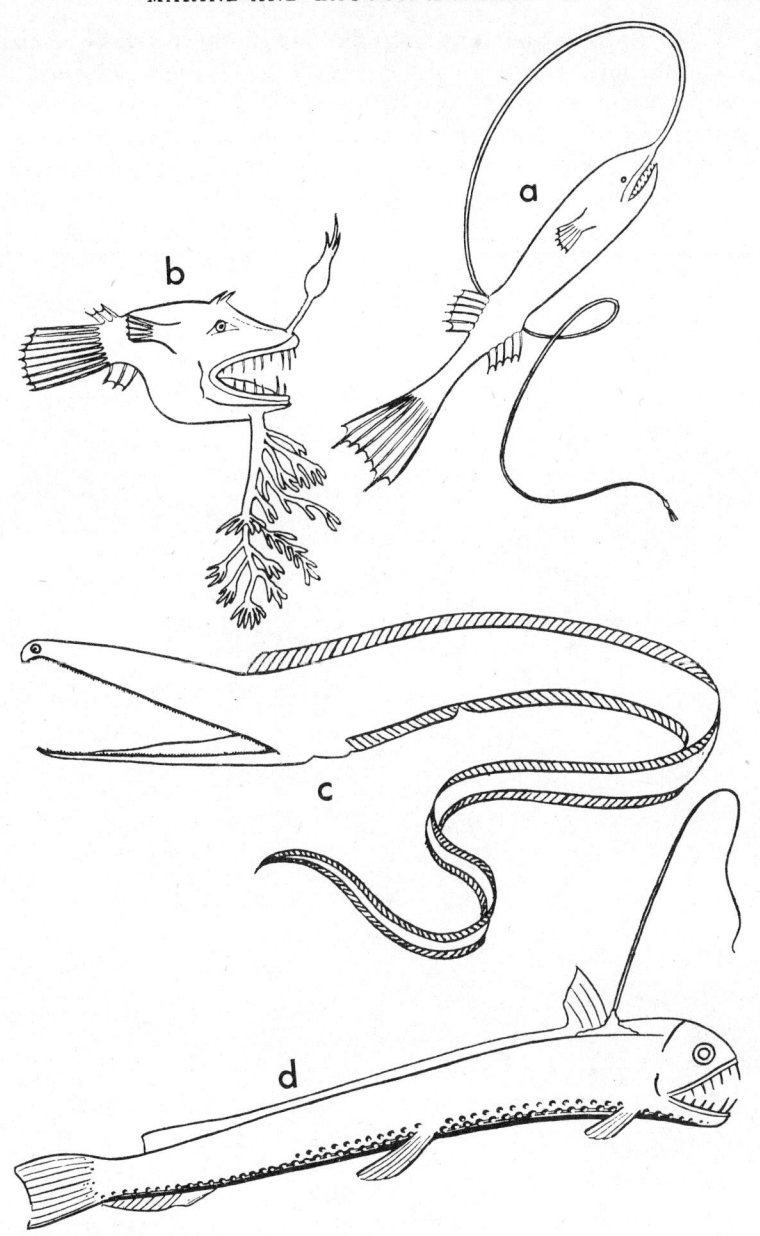

Fig. 43. Some abyssal fishes (from Hardy).

(a) *Gigantactis macronema*
(b) *Linophryne arborifer*
(c) *Eurypharynx pelicanoides*
(d) *Chauliodus sloanei*

A variety of common marine fishes are shown in Fig. 44. Among them, the most common are the **bonga fish,** *Ethmalosa fimbriata,* the **herring** *Sardinella aurita,* the **croaker** *Pseudotolithus aurita,* the **sea catfish** *Arius heudilotii,* and the **threadfin** *Pentanemus quinquarius.*

Sardinella and *Ethmalosa* are more or less restricted to shallow waters and estuaries where they are fished mainly from canoes. It is thus difficult to estimate annual production. Nevertheless, these fishes are clearly the mainstay of coastal fishing communities and are a familiar sight in any coastal West African market. Table IV shows landings of 7 major species of Fisheries in Lagos in 1960.

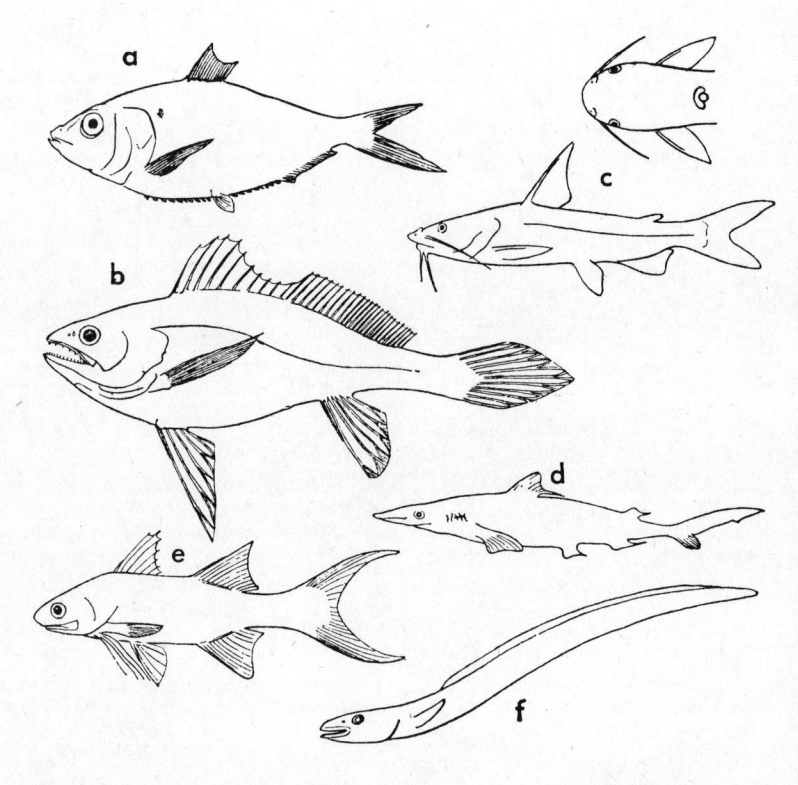

Fig. 44. Common

(a) *Ethmalosa fimbriata* (bonga fish)
(b) *Pseudotolithus aurita* (croaker)
(c) *Arius heudilotii* (sea catfish)
(d) *Scoliodon terra-novae* (shark)
(e) *Pentanemus quinquarius* (thread fish)
(f) *Conger conger* (conger-eel)

Abyssal nekton

Nektonic animals of the deep sea deserve a brief mention for the sake of completeness. The characteristic features of deep-water nekton include the development of **light organs** on strategic parts of their bodies, the development of very large mouths with various devices for attracting prey into them, and their rather curious shapes shown in Fig. 43.

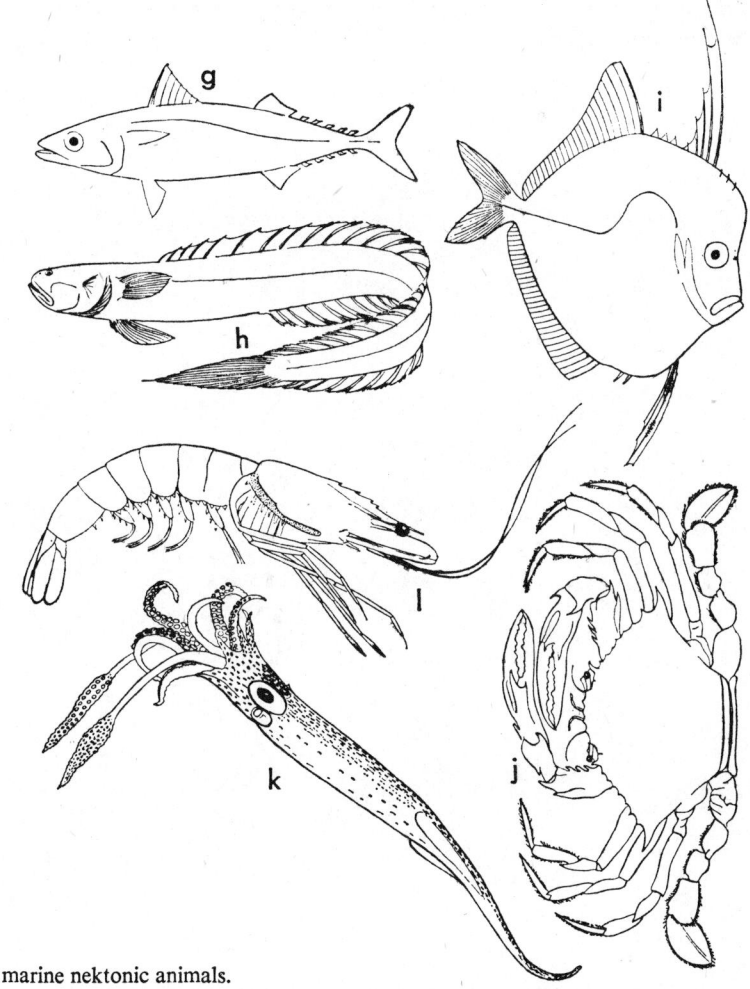

marine nektonic animals.

(*g*) *Scomber sp.* (mackerel)
(*h*) *Gobioides ansorgii* (goby)
(*i*) *Vomer setipinnis* (moon fish)
(*j*) *Callinectes gladiator* (marine swimming crab)
(*k*) *Liligo sp.* (squid)
(*l*) *Penaeus duorarum* (marine prawn)

It is doubtful whether these light organs actually help the animals to find their way in the total darkness of the abyss but it is more likely that other animals will be attracted to them. Within recent years, a craft known as the bathyscaphe has enabled man to descend to depths previously thought impossible, and perhaps it will not be long before we have a greater knowledge of the mode of life of these abyssal animals.

The lagoon nekton

A number of fishes listed as marine forms are sufficiently euryhaline and are to be found also in brackish water. *Ethmalosa* and *Arius*, for example, are well represented in the lagoons; and among the prawns, *Parapenaeopsis atlantica* is found in brackish water, whereas the marine prawn *Penaeus duorarum* is not, except during early growth.

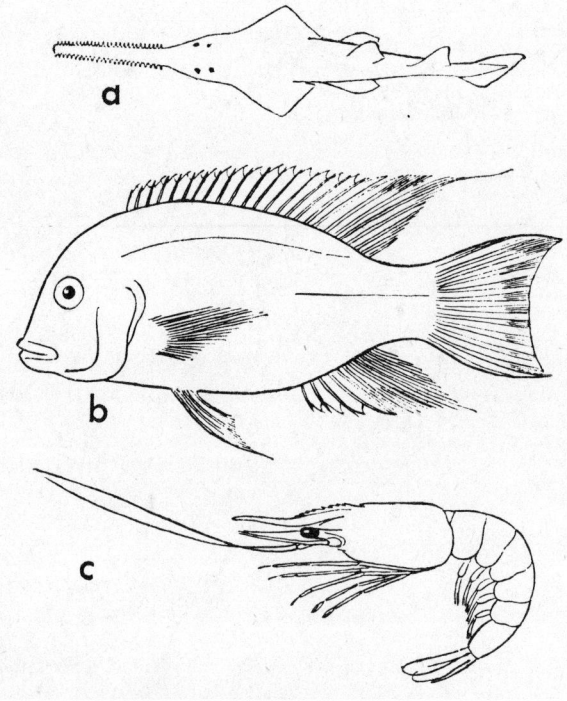

Fig. 45. Some lagoon nekton.
(a) *Pristis* (The saw fish)
(b) *Tilapia melanopleura*
(c) *Parapenaeopsis atlantica* (brackish water prawn)

On the whole, the ability to tolerate salinity change has not been developed among the chondrichthyes—the group to which the dogfish belongs—so that almost all the fishes in brackish water are bony. A few, however, such as the saw-fish *Pristis*, have been able to do this, although it is quite a rare find in lagoons, and it makes news every time one is caught. One catch which made news in 1961 was said to have inflicted such injuries on the fisherman that he died in hospital a few days later. From its common name, and by looking at Fig. 45(*a*) you can visualize how the fish might have caused this fatal accident. Other common fishes in the lagoon are various species of the cichlid fish *Tilapia*. This is predominantly a freshwater family in Africa and comprises several species. The common species found in different parts of the lagoon are *Tilapia melanopleura* and *Tilapia heudeloti*. It is difficult to distinguish these from each other, at least for a beginner, but it is easy to differentiate a cichlid from most other fish by its two lateral lines shown in Fig. 45(*b*).

Tilapias are of great economic value, forming an important part of the lagoon fisheries. In addition, they are useful for mosquito control as they are known to devour mosquito eggs and larvae with relish. Some species have also become famous for their habit of incubating eggs in their mouths, but this aspect of their behaviour will be more appropriately dealt with in Chapter 7 where *Tilapias* will be considered as part of the freshwater fauna.

Things to do

(i) *Plankton collection*. During a visit to sea or lagoon, plankton should be collected. Filtering water through a suitable hand net will give a satisfactory collection for class use, but if a boat or canoe with outboard motor is available a proper haul will produce more interesting results. The net should be hauled just below the surface in order to avoid floating debris entering the net. A five- to ten-minute haul suffices. The live plankton should be investigated immediately, using a lens, and later preserved in 4% formalin for further study in the laboratory.

(ii) *Visit to a fishing village*. All along the coast, fishing villages are to be found. As fishing tends to be seasonal, a visit should be planned for the dry season, when there is most activity. Fishing methods in the different villages may vary, but by their dissemination from one community to another more uniform methods are beginning to emerge. On the whole, the migratory fishermen from Ghana have been responsible for introducing their methods of using large seine nets operated from the beach to various parts of West Africa. Methods used in different localities should be studied and catches investigated and compared.

(iii) *Sea trip on fishing trawler.* If this can be arranged, it should be a fascinating trip for everyone—if the weather is good! This can often be arranged with the fisheries department in your area or with a local fishing company.

The following could be of interest during such a trip:

- (*a*) **Echo sounder.** This is an instrument which gives a continuous recording of the depth of the water by sending sound signals which are reflected from the bottom.
- (*b*) Measurement of temperature at different depths.
- (*c*) Use of nets for surface and deep-water fishing for plankton and fishes.

To avoid sea sickness, tablets prescribed by a competent chemist may be taken.

(iv) *Visit to a fish market.* If none of the above is possible, then a visit to a fish market could be valuable. It is essential to differentiate between marine and freshwater fishes by making enquiry as to their origin from the market women. It is advisable not to handle the fishes and to indicate from the start that your interest is scientific and not gastronomic.

(v) *Marine aquarium.* This is difficult to keep as it requires constant pumping of sea water and efficient aeration. Marine invertebrates may be kept alive for short periods in tanks of sea water.

7: Freshwater animals

Unlike the marine habitat, freshwater is easily accessible for study, since most streams, rivers, lakes, ponds, and even small puddles left after heavy rain contain some forms of freshwater animals. The features of a freshwater habitat and the characteristics of freshwater animals have already been considered in Chapter 4, where it was noted that, except for osmoregulation, the requirements of freshwater animals are similar in many respects to those of marine animals.

You already know the two types of freshwater habitats, lotic and lentic, but it is important to realize that, as in most classifications, these cannot be sharp divisions. The important factor is the speed of the water current, and since this varies a great deal there is bound to be a gradation from sluggish streams which closely resemble lentic waters to swift streams. We can also produce a change from lotic to lentic conditions. When a dam is built across a river, for example, a lentic zone is produced within the course of normally lotic waters. Such a change has been effected on the Volta river in Ghana, and on the River Niger at Kainji, in Nigeria. Fortunately, studies of fauna and flora were carried out before the dams were completed. Now that the lakes are established, interesting studies continue and comparison of fauna and flora before and after is possible.

Lentic freshwater animals (Fauna of lakes and reservoirs)

Beginning with the littoral zone, the most easily accessible part, you will find that any collection includes a variety of animals, but consists mainly of insect larvae. Some live on the substratum, some are planktonic, while others live on the partly or fully submerged plants which are a common feature of most freshwater habitats. There is some evidence from studies in other parts of the world that the last group of animals exhibit a type of *zonation* associated with the zonation of the plants on which they live. From the shallow edge to the deeper waters of the littoral zone (see Fig. 3) a zonation of plants is often evident, and the animals on one type of plant may differ from those on the others. However, most of the animals occur, more or less all over the littoral

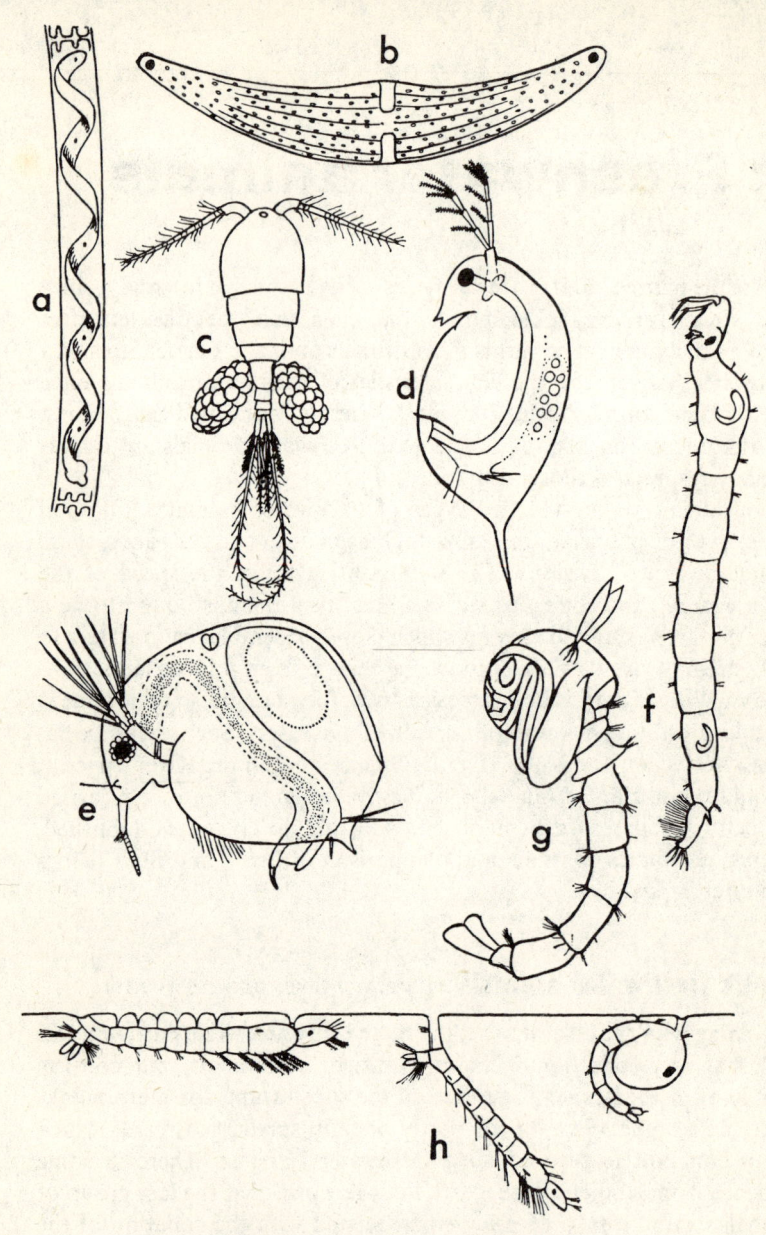

Fig. 46. Lentic freshwater plankton.

(a) *Spirogyra sp.*
(b) *Closterium* (a desmid)
(c) *Cyclops sp.*
(d) *Daphnia sp.*
(e) *Bosmina sp.*
(f) *Chaoborus* larva
(g) *Chaoborus* pupa
(h) Mosquito larvae and pupa

zone, and it is best to deal with the groups one by one, beginning with the planktonic.

The phytoplankton includes various algae and diatoms similar in form to those of the sea. In addition, filamentous forms such as *Spirogyra* and various blue-green algae are most common, often forming a thick green floating or submerged scum in the littoral zone. When diatoms predominate a brownish colour results. The zooplankton consists mainly of crustacea and the most common animals are the copepods, especially of the genus *Diaptomus* and *Cyclops*, and the Cladocera, of the genus *Daphnia* and *Bosmina*. Freshwater medusae such as *Limnocnida* sometimes occur. Unlike the marine plankton, larval forms are not abundant. In fact, many freshwater animals seem to have developed ways of avoiding the larval stage. One of the reasons for this is that the freshwater habitat is a less favourable one than the sea. In freshwater, if an animal hatches at a mature stage, it stands a better chance of survival than a larval stage. Furthermore the larva would be in greater danger of being swept away in the running water of rivers and streams. A planktonic larva which deserves special mention is the larva of the midge fly *Chaoborus*. This larva is found in most freshwaters and is not restricted to surface waters. It is one of the planktonic organisms usually found near the bottom in the hypolimnion zone, but it is capable of vertical migration. The four air sacs, two at each end of the body, are quite prominent. These assure the animal of adequate oxygen supply whilst in the hypolimnion.

The animals which attach themselves to the vegetation, or hold on temporarily, are rather difficult to separate from the plankton, or from the bottom fauna, as they occur in both types of collection. In some books, they are classed together as the *periphyton*. Among them are various insect larvae such as **dragon fly nymphs, May fly nymphs, pond snails, water mites, flatworms, rotifers,** and **hydroids**. Representatives of these groups are shown in Fig. 47. Some of them, such as the snails, feed on the plants, to which they are attached, whilst others are carnivorous or planktonic feeders. Among the carnivores are the various species of dragon fly nymphs which have a well-developed labium for catching prey. When not in use, this organ partly covers the face of the animal, hence it is called a mask. Flatworms are also carnivorous, everting their pharynx to devour the food. A way to collect them is simply to leave some meat in a bottle in a running stream at some convenient position.

Among the bottom dwellers are various **annelid worms, blood worms, snails, nymphs,** and other burrowing forms. The bottom of lentic freshwaters is usually muddy because fine particles of silt tend to settle

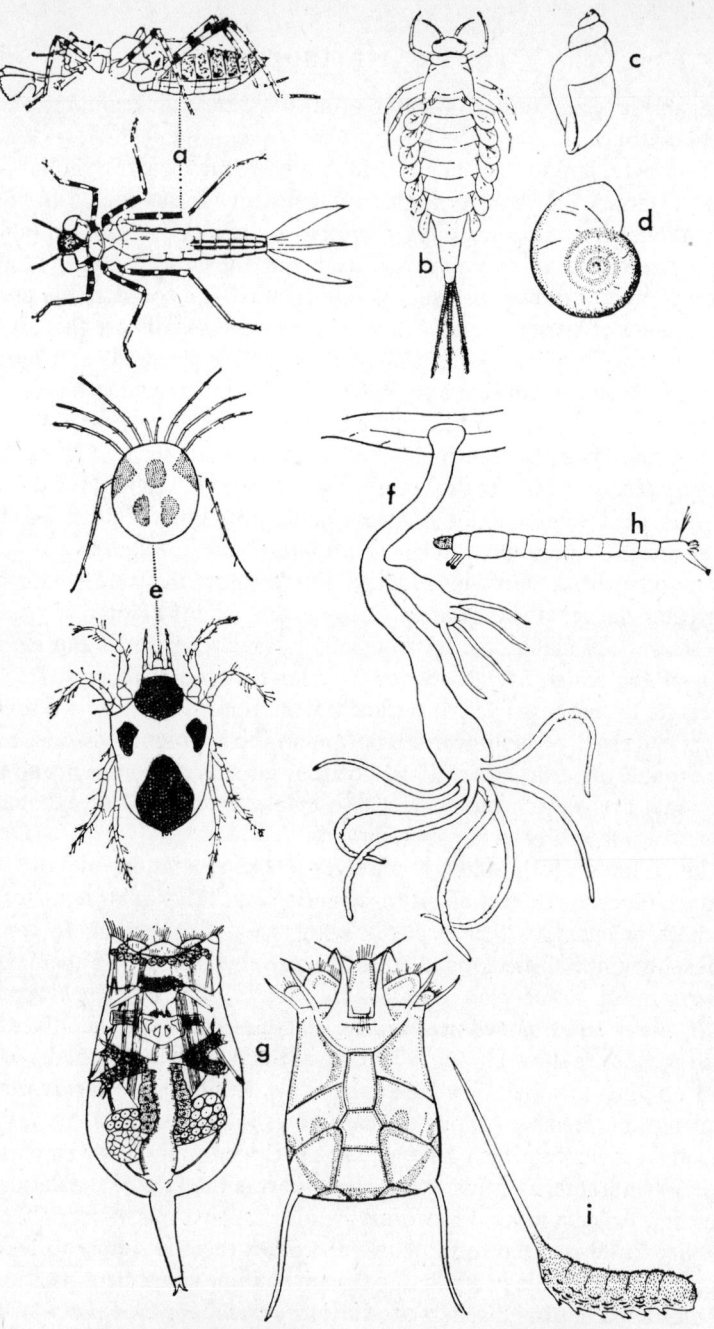

Fig. 47. Lentic freshwater periphyton and benthic animals.

(a) Dragon fly nymph; bottom and climbing types
(b) May fly nymph
(c) Pond snail, *Limnaea truncatula*
(d) Pond snail, *Planorbis sp.*
(e) Water mites
(f) *Hydra sp.*
(g) Rotifers
(h) *Chironomus* larva
(i) *Eristalis* larva

in enclosed waters, and a sample from the bottom yields a good number of these organisms. Generally, the bottom fauna in deep water is poor because of lack of adequate food and oxygen. The animals found here therefore are those which feed on detritus, and those which have adaptations for living in water with low oxygen concentration. Blood worms in particular are common. These are not annelids, as the common name tends to suggest, but the larvae of a dipteran fly, more correctly named *chironomus larvae*. The red colour is due to the presence of haemoglobin in the blood, an adaptation for living in muddy bottoms with low oxygen concentration. A different method is adopted by the rat-tailed larva of *Eristalis*. This larva is a shallow bottom dweller, and has a long extensible siphon reaching up to the surface for obtaining atmospheric oxygen.

We must now consider the nektonic organisms. The first nektonic animals you are likely to observe are those which live on the surface, supported by the water film. The long-legged **pond skaters,** *Gerris sp.*, moving elegantly with great ease on the surface of the water attract the attention of even the most casual observer. Another common animal is the **whirligig beetle,** *Gyrinus sp.*, which has an interesting adaptation for life on the water film by the division of the eye into two halves, one half used below the water surface and the other above.

Below the water surface, there are various types of small diving-invertebrate animals, chief among them being the diving beetle *Dytiscus*, and the back swimmer *Notonecta*. Others, shown in Fig. 48, are the water scorpion *Nepa*, and the giant water bug *Belostoma*. In spite of leading an aquatic life, all these animals use atmospheric oxygen and are therefore adapted for this in one of two ways. First, some are able to carry air bubbles entrapped in fine hairs on their body, or between the body and the wings, which they use whilst remaining below water surface for long periods. Any of these animals with a fresh supply of air can be easily distinguished by its silvery appearance which is gradually reduced as the air bubble is used up. A second method is by the development of breathing siphons which project through the water surface so that the animal can remain below the surface during intake of air. A long type of siphon found in the bottom dwelling *eristalis larva* has already been mentioned. A rather shorter type is shown in *Nepa*, while the larvae and pupae of mosquitoes also come into this category.

Before going on to the fishes which form the bulk of the nekton of freshwater, it is important to mention the presence of amphibious vertebrates in the littoral zone. **Toads, frogs, terrapins, river turtles, crocodiles, water snakes,** and even **manatees** and **hippos** when they occur, are

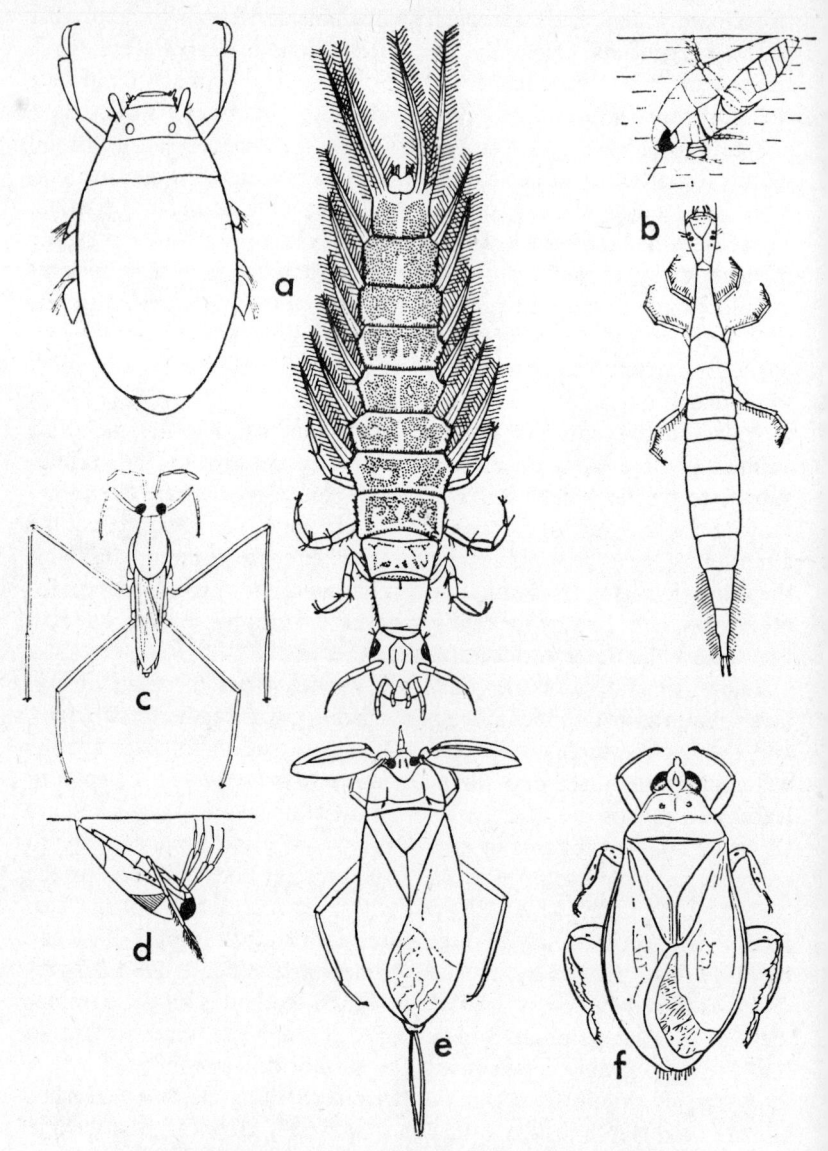

Fig. 48. Surface and diving invertebrates in lentic freshwater.

(a) *Gyrinus sp.* (whirligig beetle) adult and larva
(b) *Dytiscus sp.* (diving beetle) adult and larva
(c) *Gerris sp.* (pond skater)
(d) *Notonecta sp.* (back swimmer)
(e) *Nepa sp.* (water scorpion)
(f) *Belostoma sp.* (giant water bug)

usually found in the littoral zone, although they may seek food in deeper water. As you know, they depend entirely on atmospheric oxygen and, living in the littoral zone, they are able to surface more easily, or make excursions on to land.

Among the amphibia, two common species *Xenopus tropicalis* and *X. mulleri* show an interesting pattern of distribution, the former in forest areas and the latter in savanna. The distribution of the two species overlaps in the areas between forest and savanna as shown by a study around Ibadan in Western Nigeria. Here they have been found to occur in water holes a few feet apart but never in the same water hole. For the interested collector, *X. mulleri* has larger eyes than *X. tropicalis*, and *X. mulleri* has no spur on the metatarsal tubercle as in *X. tropicalis*.

A full description of freshwater fishes would constitute a major work by itself. All that can be included in the limited space available is a list of the more common ones found in our freshwaters. Although the lung fish *Protopterus annectens* is found only in a few areas of West Africa it is included as a representative of a primitive but interesting group of fishes which possess a lung and internal nostrils.

Two other primitive fishes worth mention are the sail fish *Polypterus*

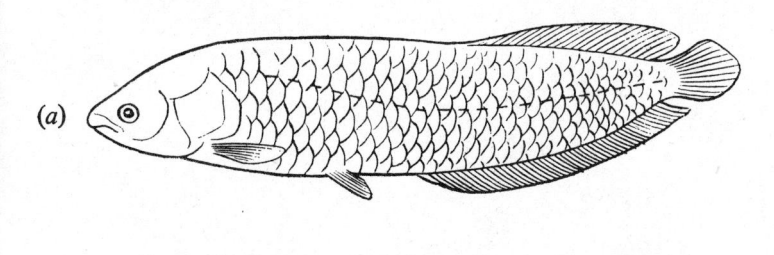

Fig. 49. Nesting behaviour of *Heterotis niloticus*.
(a) *Heterotis niloticus* (b) *Heterotis niloticus* in its nest

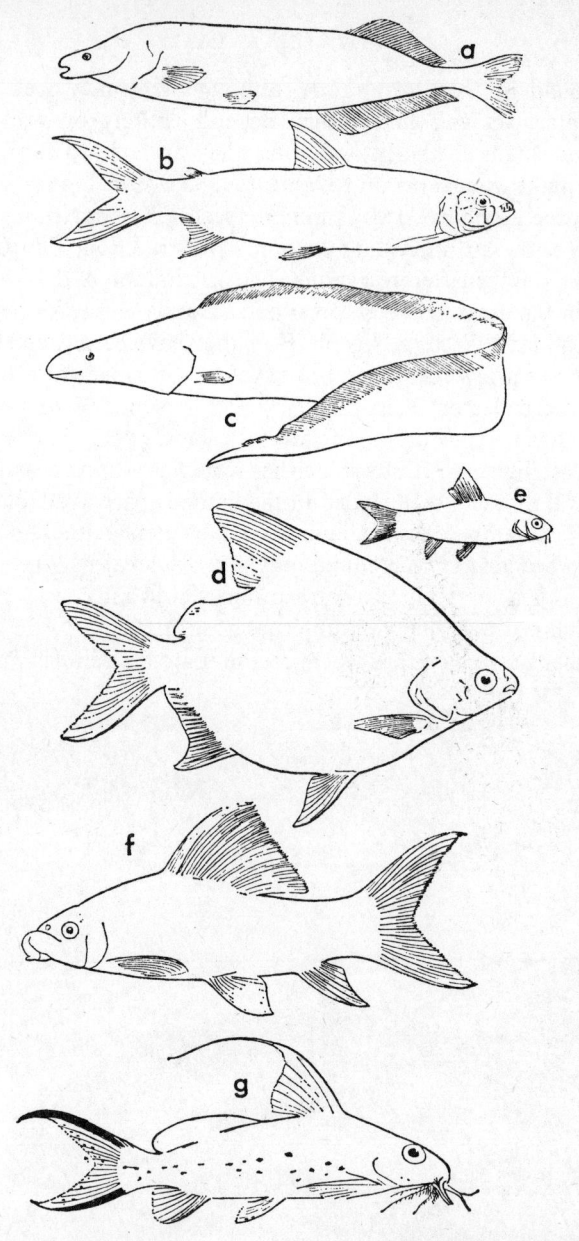

Fig. 50. Some common

(a) *Mormyrops sp.* (snout fish)
(b) *Hydrocyon sp.* (tiger fish)
(c) *Gymnachus niloticus*
(d) *Citharinus latus* (moon fish)
(e) *Barbus nigeriensis* (barbel)
(f) *Labeo coubie* (African carp)
(g) *Synodontis filamentosa* (cat fish)

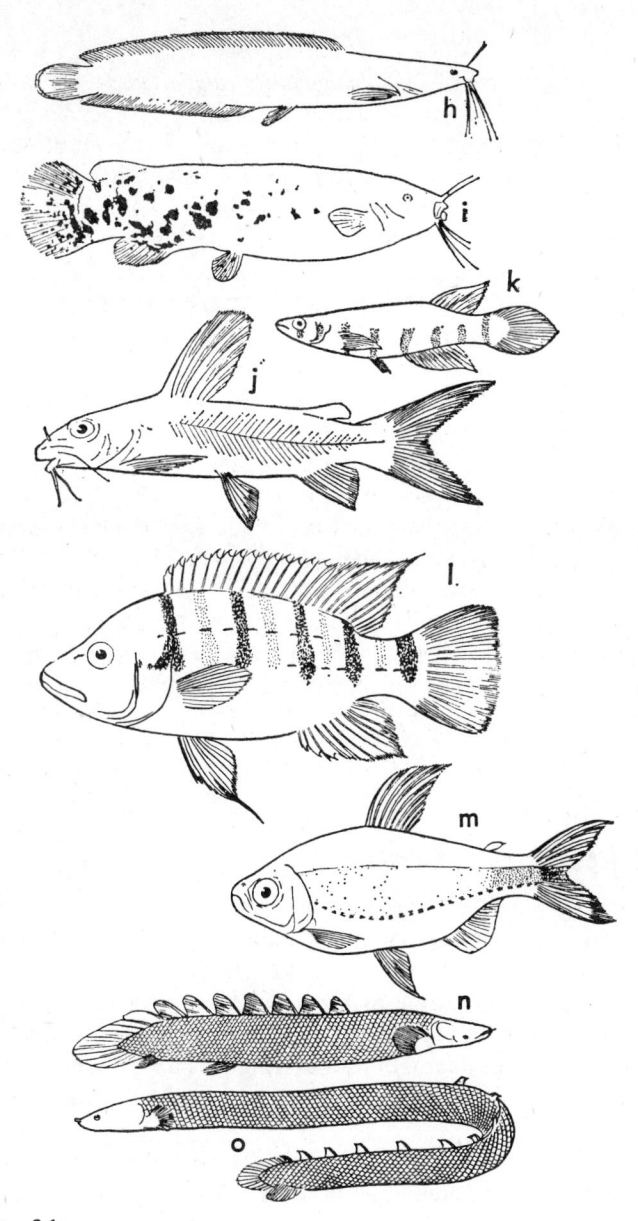

freshwater fishes.

(h) *Clarias anguillaris* (mud fish)
(i) *Malopterurus electricus* (electric cat fish)
(j) *Chrysichthys nigrodigitatus* (cat fish)
(k) *Epiplatys sexfasciatus*
(l) *Hemichromis fasciatus*
(m) *Alestes longispini* (characin)
(n) *Polypterus senegalus* (sail fish)
(o) *Calamoichthys calabaricus* (reed fish)

senegalus and the reed fish *Calamoichthys calabaricus*; these both have bony scales which do not overlap as is common in other bony fishes.

Among the modern bony fishes (Figs. 49 and 50) the mouth-breeding fish *Tilapia* and the nest-building fish *Heterotis niloticus*, because of their special breeding habits, deserve special mention.

As was pointed out whilst dealing with lagoon nekton, there are many different species of *Tilapia*, and *T. heudeloti* and *T. melanopleura* were mentioned as typical lagoon forms. The common freshwater types in West Africa, *T. galilaea* and *T. nilotica*, attain larger sizes than the lagoon forms. As their specific names imply, they are found all over Africa, the specific name *galilaea* refers to Galilee of biblical fame, and *nilotica* to the River Nile. Of these tilapias *T. galilaea* and *T. heudeloti* are known to incubate their eggs in their mouths, where, after hatching them, they retain the young for some length of time. This is a form of parental care found only among the cichlids. (See Plates IV and V.)

Parental care in *Heterotis niloticus* is of a different kind. It builds a nest of grass in shallow water and keeps its young protected in this nest for about a week. It breaches the nest to release the young and continues to protect them for a couple of months afterwards. This care is essential for the young, for if they are transferred to another pond, or their parent is transferred before they reach a particular size, they fail to survive.

Lotic freshwater animals

In lotic freshwater, the speed of the water seems to be the primary factor which determines the type of animals present. In the **pool zone** where the water moves very slowly, the physical characteristics of the area are virtually the same as for lentic waters; whereas in the **rapids zone** this is not so. It only remains for us to consider the fauna in the rapids zone, and the adaptations which animals have developed to cope with water currents, varying from that in an average stream to that over falls or rapids.

Most inhabitants of lotic waters have a streamlined body, that is, rather elongated and pointed at both ends, which reduces water resistance. This, of course, is an adaptation for all aquatic habitats and not only lotic waters. Dorso-ventral flattening to enable closer attachment to the substratum and consequently less danger of being swept by the current is also common. Flatworms, and a number of nymphs show this adaptation well. Usually associated with dorso-ventral flattening is a

FRESHWATER ANIMALS 111

physiological adaptation known as **thigmotaxis,** the tendency to cling to surfaces. This is an inborn behaviour pattern of advantage in fast-flowing lotic waters. You will remember that some animals of the intertidal zone such as the rock crabs had a similar adaptation. In view of the fact that the problem of holding on requires to be solved by animals in both niches, it is not surprising that the same sort of adaptations have been evolved.

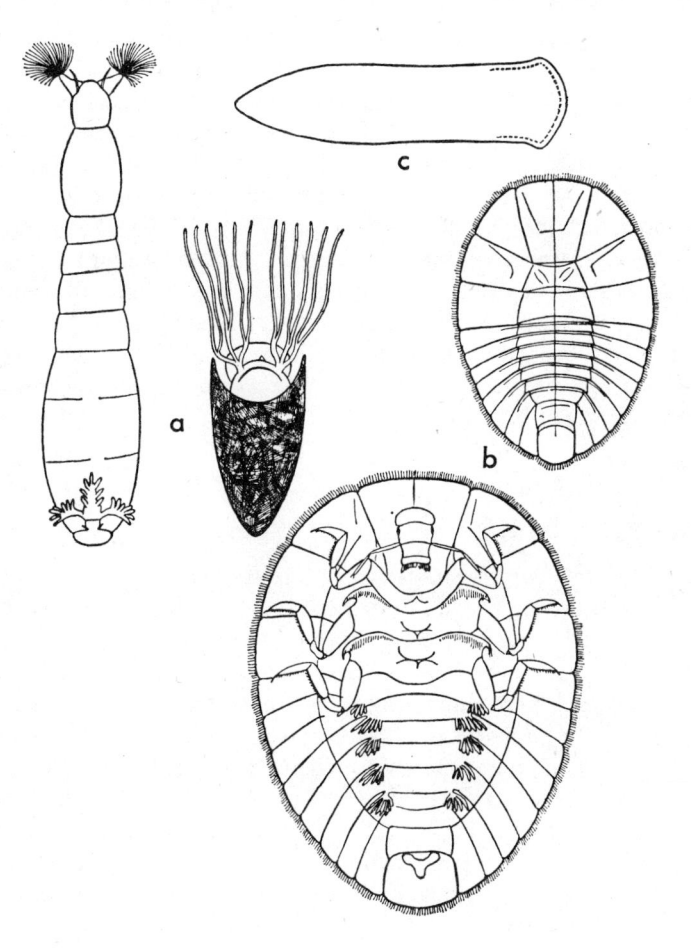

Fig. 51. Some animals of the rapids zone of lotic freshwater.

(a) *Simulium* larva and pupa
(b) Flattened nymph of riffle beetle (water penny) dorsal and ventral
(c) *Polycelis sp.* (polyclad turbellarian)

Another type of adaptation is the development of attachment organs, varying from temporary attachment by use of mucous secretions, adopted by snails and flatworms, and the use of hooks and suckers by some insect larvae, to permanent attachment to the substratum found in the freshwater oysters amongst the mollusca. The larva of the insect *Simulium* not only has hooks and suckers for attachment, but also a silk **safety rope**, so that if swept off its hold it can safely find its way back. The pupal stage also develops a cocoon which is attached to the rock surface. A similar adaptation is found in the larvae of some caddis flies.

An interesting physiological adaptation in some animals of lotic waters is the ability to orientate themselves in the appropriate direction and swim with or against the current. It has been shown that animals found in lentic freshwaters do not possess this ability, often referred to as **rheotaxis**. When swimming against the current it is *positive rheotaxis*, and when with the current *negative rheotaxis*. Some fishes have the habit of swimming upstream to lay their eggs, often jumping waterfalls and rapids. After laying their eggs, they swim in the opposite direction. In such fishes, rheotactic behaviour is closely linked with reproduction. This type of behaviour is also found in the common freshwater prawn *Palaemon paucidens*, and it is probably a common characteristic of many animals of lotic waters.

Freshwater birds

Before closing our consideration of the freshwater habitat we must take note that a number of birds feed and breed in such places. These include many forms that are migrant to West Africa, notably **ducks, herons,** and **waders;** and also many others that remain throughout the year. Aquatic birds show interesting adaptations; some, like the **grebes** and the **fin-foot** *Podica senegalensis*, have fleshy lobes along the toes to form a more effective swimming paddle, while ducks and **pelicans** have a complete web between the toes. The **Lily-trotter** *Actophilornis africana* has very long toes that enable it to support its weight while walking over floating vegetation. The herons have long legs for wading into the water in search of their prey. Aquatic birds often have specialized beaks for dealing with their food. Thus the fish-eating **kingfishers** have a strong spear-like beak, the **Skimmer** *Rhynchops flavirostris* has the lower mandible longer than the upper one to enable it to collect surface water plankton, and the **flamingoes** have a curiously bent bill and pumping tongue mechanism that enables them to

FRESHWATER ANIMALS 113

sweep up algae and plankton from near the bottom in shallow water. Many of these aquatic birds build their nests over water in the shelter of the surrounding reeds, and the *grebes* even build floating nests.

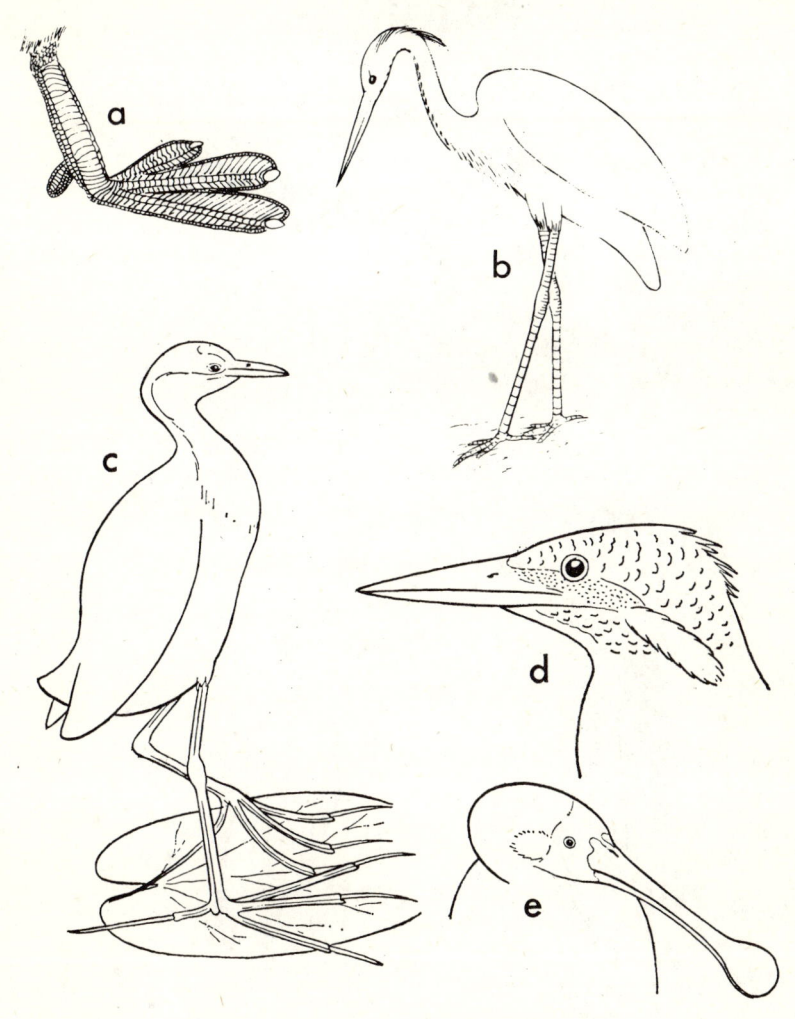

Fig. 52. Adaptation for aquatic life in birds.

(a) Webbed foot of Crested Grebe *Podiceps cristatus*
(b) Feet of heron *Typhon goliath*
(c) *Actophilornis africana* (Common Lily Trotter)
(d) Head of Giant Kingfisher *Megaceryle maxima*
(e) Head of African Spoonbill *Platalea alba*

T A E—E

Fig. 53. Some shore and freshwater birds.
(a) *Actitis hypoleucos* (Sand Piper)
(b) *Chlidonias nigra* (Black Tern)
(c) *Rhynchops flavirostris* (Skimmer)
(d) *Pelecanus sp.* (Pelican)
(e) *Oceanites oceanicus* (Wilson's Petrel)
(f) *Concomer vocifer* (West African Sea Eagle)

A great deal remains to be studied about our freshwaters and their fauna. With the relatively easier accessibility to freshwater, it is surprising that not much more is known at present. It is hoped that more people will take an interest in the collection and study of freshwater animals so that knowledge about them will increase.

Things to do

(i) *Collecting*. The methods for collecting in a marine habitat are equally applicable in freshwater. The animal population of a lentic freshwater should be studied, carefully noting the distribution of animals on the weeds and grasses at the edge, on submerged plants, and on floating plants. Compare your collections noting any zonation.

In a similar way, animals in lotic water should be studied. Collections should be made in different parts such as over a culvert, where the water runs fast; over a muddy bottom, rocky bottom, or sandy bottom.

Also make collections of planktonic and bottom fauna, using plankton net and scraper net respectively.

(ii) *Freshwater aquarium*. It is most desirable to have a couple of freshwater aquaria in which common fishes can be kept. About the easiest to keep are the tilapias. To keep an aquarium properly some books on the subject should be consulted. The most important point to remember is that bits of food and faeces should not be left to rot in the tank thereby fouling it. Any left-overs of food should be removed from the tank with a pipette. A sand bottom and a few rocks will do for many fishes. Other fishes which can be easily kept are *Barbus*, *Epiplatys*, and *Clarias*. Aeration of the tank is not essential in keeping these fishes.

(iii) *Fish pond*. If a suitable stream passes through the school grounds a fish pond may be constructed by making a dam. For this, the permission and advice of a fisheries officer in the area will be necessary. He will advise on construction, stocking, and its general care.

(iv) *Visit to market*. Periodic visits to the local market to observe fishes (both fresh and dried) on display could be rewarding. Note any seasonal variation in abundance of major species. Also enquire about prices as this may give an indication of fluctuation in abundance as well. Prices are controlled by the simple law of supply and demand.

8: Land animals

In considering land animals, one is very much reminded that ecology is a biological subject. As was mentioned previously, floral and faunal maps within a region are very similar to each other.

The world is divided into six faunal regions called zoogeographical regions; and within each region are floral and faunal zones. Within the Ethiopian region to which West Africa belongs, the major zones of the terrestrial habitat are, Rain forest, savanna, montane and semi-desert.

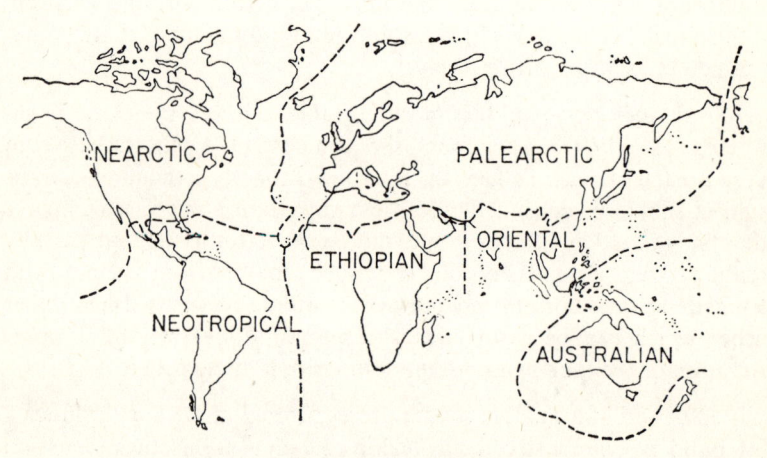

Fig. 54. Zoogeographical regions of the world.

It is important to realize that the zoogeographical regions of today, the zones within them, and their flora and fauna have reached their present state after a succession of changes since prehistoric times. In fact, there is clear evidence that the present land masses themselves have not always had their present form and position. Changes which have occurred have been due mainly to climatic factors such as temperature and humidity. Furthermore, limitations in distribution of flora and fauna have been brought about by the appearance of ecological barriers such as mountains, rivers, oceans, and deserts. Man himself has played an important part in bringing about changes in distribution in more recent times.

Even in their present form, the distribution of land animals is controlled by a number of factors such as **their rate of dispersal,** powers of **migration,** as well as **intraspecific and interspecific competition.** One of the theories which seek to explain how animals and plants have been dispersed over the surface of the earth suggests that the present-day continents were at some time more closely connected but later *drifted* to their present positions. This is the theory of *continental drift* in which two great land masses, a northern **Laurasia** and a southern **Gondwana,** are postulated. These are just mentioned in passing, as further discussion of this aspect of ecology known as zoogeography would lead to an unnecessarily long digression.

The zoogeographical region of most interest to us, Africa, south of the Sahara desert, is known as the *Ethiopian region.* It is interesting to note that this nomenclature, which has no political origin, is in keeping with the status of Ethiopia as the oldest state in Africa.

Behavioural aspects of ecology

Another branch of ecology which can only be briefly mentioned is its behavioural aspect. Protective coloration which falls within this branch of ecology has been considered in Chapter 4. The second behavioural aspect of ecology to be mentioned is *territorial behaviour;* a habit which has been studied in many land animals, especially birds. Within an area called its territory, an individual, usually a male, wards off other members of the species by various forms of aggressive pose and sometimes by fighting. This has been worked out in detail in the robin, a common European bird, but an investigation of the territorial behaviour of the rainbow lizard *Agama agama*, one of the commonest animals in most parts of West Africa, has recently been made. It was found possible to delimit the territories for marked male lizards by the use of models painted in the colours of the male rainbow lizard, and fitted so that its body could be bobbed up and down by the manipulation of a string, thus simulating the challenge posture of an intruder. Within each territory, three zones were distinguished on the following basis:

(i) A zone in which the model was actually attacked in more than 50% of trials.
(ii) A zone in which the model was challenged and threatened in more than 50% of the trials but rarely attacked.

(iii) A zone in which the model was challenged but rarely approached in more than 50% of trials.

Beyond these zones an outer boundary was mapped by watching the farthest limits of the lizard's wanderings. This interesting investigation has left one in no doubt of territorial behaviour in the rainbow lizard. Functionally the main advantage of territory in this animal seems to be the securing of a mate during the breeding season; it also ensures an adequate food supply at other times.

We shall now consider the animals of the different floral and faunal zones of West Africa, beginning with the Forest Zone.

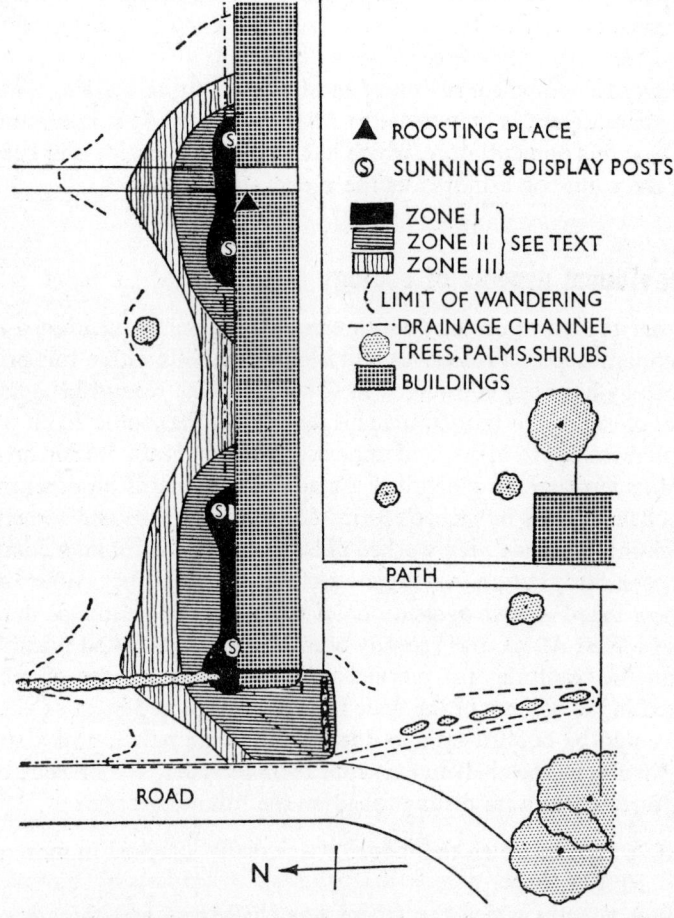

Fig. 55. Territory of a male *Agama agama* in Ibadan in February, 1957 (after Harris).

Forest animals

The Forest zone in West Africa consists of a coastal belt stretching from Sierra Leone to the Congo, except for a narrow break between Ghana and Nigeria known as the **Dahomey Gap**. The forest zone is often divided into subzones; the chief being a coastal **mangrove forest**, especially around lagoons and estuaries, followed by a true **high forest**, and thirdly, there is a **dry forest** which separates the high forest from the savanna. Finally, along streams and rivers, there are narrow incursions of forest into the savanna zone, and these are variously known as **forest outliers, fringing forest,** or **gallery forest**.

The fauna which we are about to study may be regarded as characteristic of mature forest in general; but it must be pointed out that what may be regarded as characteristic high forest or primary forest is now limited by human activity in most parts of Africa except the Congo. In West Africa, secondary forest is predominant although mature forest quite like primary forest is found in Ashanti and part of the Western Region of Ghana, and in Ijebu-Ode, Ondo, Benin, Ogoja, and Calabar Provinces of Nigeria. Details of the structure of such forest will be found in books on plant ecology.

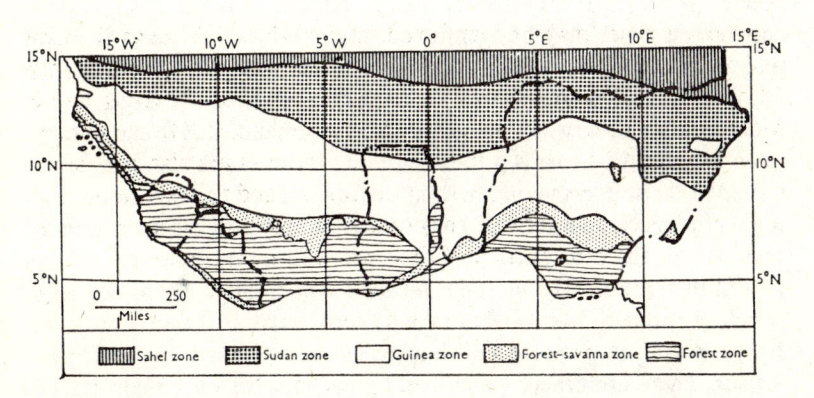

Fig. 56. Map of West Africa showing floral and faunal zones (after Keay).

One general remark concerning tropical forest fauna is about the density of its animal population. From the point of view of individuals the fauna is usually poor when compared with other types of forests; but from the point of view of number of species it is usually richer. There is also a tendency to have **giant forms** among the invertebrates and cold-blooded vertebrates in tropical forests; well-known examples are the giant beetle *Goliathus giganticus* among the coleoptera, the giant snail *Achatina* among the molluscs, and the large scorpion *Pandinus imperator*.

Forest soil fauna (See Plates VII and VIII)

Dealing first with forest soil, we find that it consists of three primary strata. First, there is a top layer of decaying leaves, humus, and worm casts known as the *litter zone,* below is the *surface soil* of variable depth, and beneath this there is the *subsoil.* In the litter zone, there are a variety of invertebrates most of which are arthropods. These include many insects such as the *collembola, ants, beetles,* and their larvae, and *mole crickets, arachnids* such as *spiders, soil mites, millipedes,* and *centipedes.* Non-arthropods include many *molluscs* and *nematodes.* Of all these the millipedes are probably the most commonly seen and, because of their slow movement, easily collected. The common large millipede *Spirostreptus assiniensis* is plentiful especially during the rains. The red smaller sized millipede *Habrodesmus flax,* which shows swarming behaviour, and the flat-shaped *Oxydesmus sp.* are also common all year round. Burrowing into the surface soil are the numerous earthworm species which leave their casts in large numbers on the surface. Two commonest types may be mentioned. *Hyperiodrilus africanus* is found mostly in the shade and is the typical forest species. It produces the familiar vertical tunnel-shaped cast. *Eudrilus euginiae* is larger and is iridescent in colour when preserved in 5% formalin. It is found in more open areas and its cast is a loose mound. Termites are also well represented in the soil, occurring both in surface soil and the subsoil depending on the species concerned. They burrow deeply and use the excavated material for the construction of their nests. Since there are no solitary types, all termites live in some form of community. There are those which continue to live in what may be considered as the ancestral way, by burrowing into wood, and having no defined nests—as in *Cryptotermes*. There are others which build giant mounds over their nests as in the large fungus-growing termite *Macrotermes bellicosus* whose mound may be up to 6 metres high. Intermediate between these are the harvester termites *Hodotermes* which build underground nests without mounds.

Materials used for the building of the nest also vary. In the genera which feed on wood and dry vegetation their excrement, which is largely of lignin, cellulose, and other vegetable products, dries to form a cardboard-like material with which the nest is constructed, and soil is added as an outer layer. In the groups of termites which feed on vegetable residue in the soil, their excrement is a mixture of fine clay and small vegetable particles, and it is this that is moulded into the thin walls of the nest. In the third group, consisting chiefly of the *Macrotermitinae*,

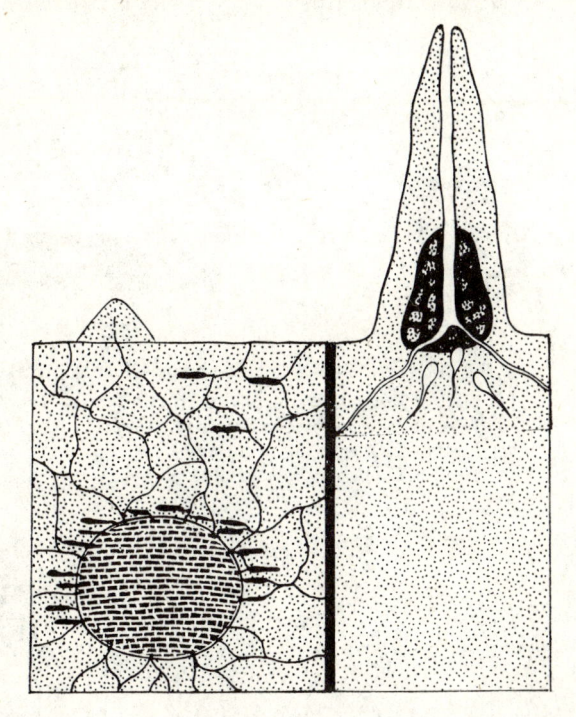

Fig. 57. Nests of *Hodotermes* (*left*) and *Macrotermes* (*right*) compared (modified from Harris).

the nest is built of sand and clay mixed with saliva. In these nests there are elaborate chambers for the queen, for growing fungus, and for nursing the young. Radiating from the nest are a complex pattern of corridors leading into surrounding country through which workers travel in search of wood for food, and soil for building.

The size and shape of mounds remain uniform for a particular species only if it is limited in distribution to a small ecological zone. When distribution is over a wide area, then other factors affect the external appearance of the mound. On the other hand, the internal arrangement of the nest remains constant. For example, in *Macrotermes bellicosus* with a distribution all over Africa, the outward appearance of the mound varies with the intensity of rainfall, and the proportion of clay

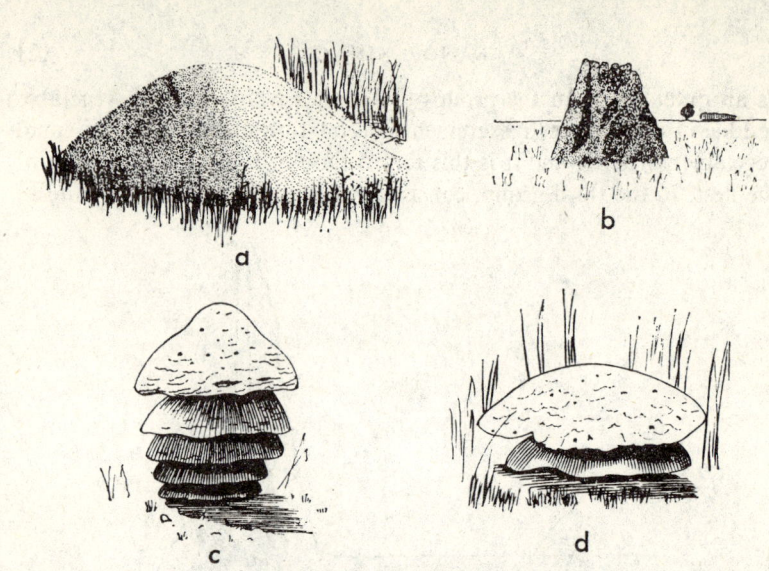

Fig. 58 Termite nests (modified from Harris).

(a) Nest of *Macrotermes bellicosus* in rain forest
(b) Nest of *Macrotermes bellicosus* in savanna
(c) Nest of *Cubitermes* in rain forest
(d) Nest of *Cubitermes* in savanna

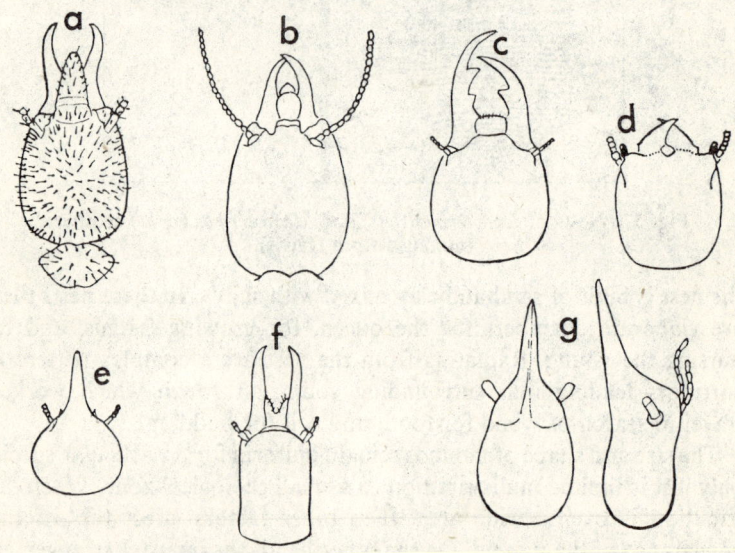

Fig. 59. Soldiers heads of common termites (from Webb).

(a) *Microtermes lepidus*
(b) *Macrotermes nigeriensis*
(c) *Hodotermes sp.*
(d) *Gryptotermes domesticus*
(e) *Nasutitermes sp.*
(f) *Cubitermes minitabundus*
(g) *Trinervetermes sp.*

LAND ANIMALS

in the subsoil. In the rain forests, the mounds are broad based and only a few metres high, whereas in the savanna they produce tall steeple-shaped mounds which are usually several metres high.

Another mound shape worthy of mention is the umbrella or pagoda type in *Cubitermis* which also occurs in both forest and savanna and varies in form in the different areas.

Mention must also be made of the arboreal nests and mounds built by species of *Nasutitermes*. They are usually of cardboard-like material, although they may be covered with earth. However high up they may be, they are really a part of the subterranean community, to which they are joined by earthen runways along the trunk of the tree.

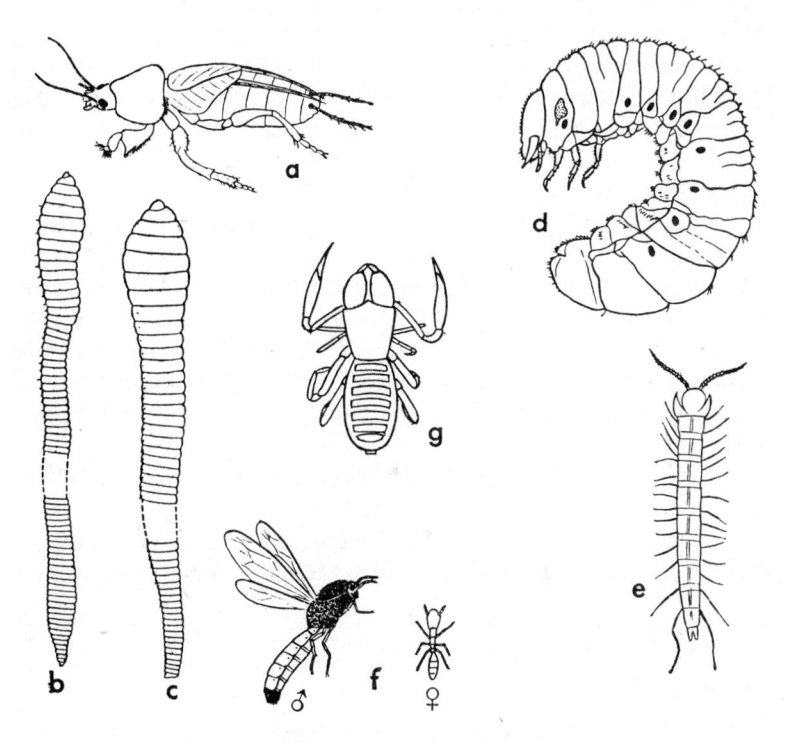

Fig. 60. More soil invertebrates.

(a) *Gryllotalpa sp.* (mole cricket)
(b) *Hyperiodrilus africanus* (earthworm)
(c) *Eudrilus euginiae* (earthworm)
(d) Larva of *Oryctes boas* (compost beetle)
(e) *Lithobius sp.* (centipede)
(f) *Dorylus helvolus* (driver ant)
(g) Pseudoscorpion (sp. unknown)

Among the ants, the common driver ant *Dorylus* is subterranean in habit, building temporary nests which it abandons after a time. One fact which is not commonly known is that the large wasplike **sausage flies** found around lamps during the early rains each year are the males of the driver ant. The driver ants are carnivorous, but most other soil invertebrates are herbivorous or detritus feeders.

Vertebrates too are found in the soil and should be considered as part of the soil fauna especially if they spend most of their time in burrows or tunnels and only leave their home to find food. Among the amphibia there are the burrowing worm-like forms known as **coecilians,** which are not common in West Africa, and only one *Herpele squalostoma* has been recorded. Any other finds would be of great value to science.

Burrowing reptiles include burrowing snakes, the largest being the **burrowing python** *Calabaria reinhardtii* which may attain a length of 1 metre. It is harmless and inoffensive, tending to roll up into a defensive ball when in danger. There is also the harmless, **worm-like snake** *Typhlops punctatus*. Unfortunately not all burrowing snakes are harmless, because they include the **burrowing vipers** *Atracaspis sp.*, which are highly poisonous.

Among burrowing mammals, the most common are the rodents. The common **pouched rat** *Cricetomys gambianus* is very well known, and although it is found in the savanna it is more common in forest. *Cricetomys* spends most of the day in its burrow which usually has many exits, thus enabling it to escape in time of danger. *Cricetomys* is hunted by both young and old in rural areas, and everyone knows that the usual procedure is first to find and block all the tunnel exits before smoking out of the animal is commenced.

The **otter shrew** *Potamogale velox* lives in burrows on the banks of streams and rivers, emerging at night to feed in the water. It has not been recorded very often west of Cameroon, but being nocturnal and aquatic it is not surprising that its distribution is so poorly known.

Forest ground dwellers

Above ground, the distribution of animals may be considered to be in two parts: there is the fauna of *forest floor,* and above this the arboreal fauna. The latter may show subdivisions corresponding with the lower, middle, and upper *storeys* of vegetation, depending on the maturity of the forest. Each of these vertical zones has its own characteristic fauna.

On the forest floor, the common invertebrates are difficult to separate

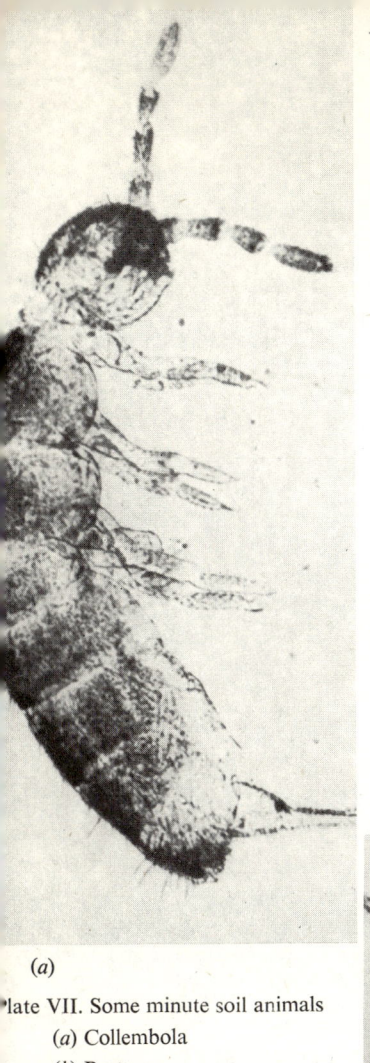

(a)

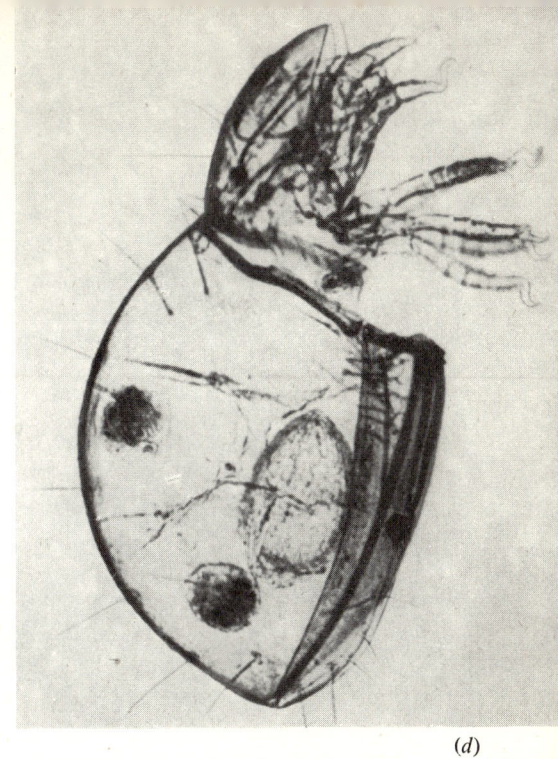

(b)

(c)

(d)

Plate VII. Some minute soil animals
(a) Collembola
(b) Protura
(c), (d) Soil mites

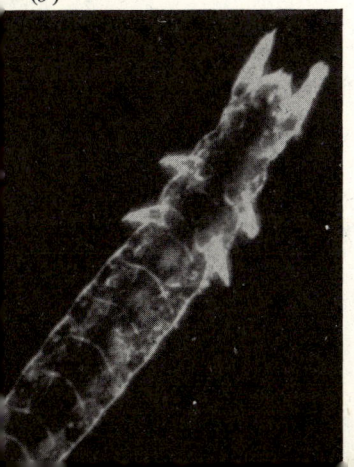

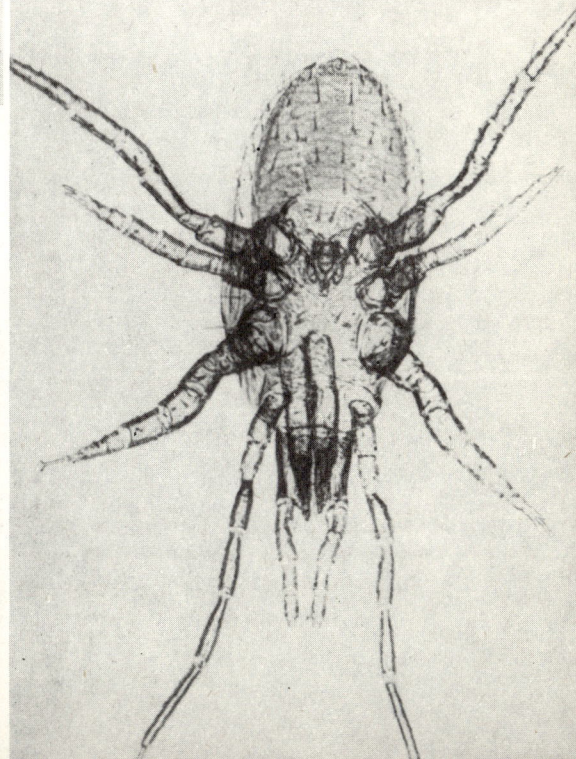

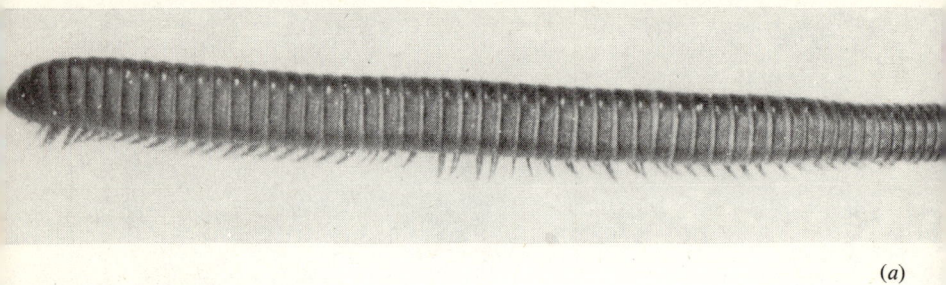

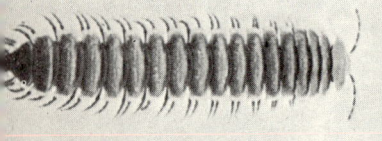

Plate VIII. Common millipedes of forest soil
(a) *Spirostreptus assiniensis*
(b) *Oxydesmus sp*
(c) *Habrodesmus flax*
(d) Swarming behaviour of *Habrodesmus*

from those of the litter zone of the soil. They consist mainly of ants, the **army ants** being characteristic. These are mostly carnivorous, the army ant *Anomma nigricans* being particularly ferocious and nomadic, organizing themselves into marching columns for hunting expeditions.

Apart from ants, coleoptera and diptera are also well represented. Amphibia are common on the forest floor especially near water courses. Among the frogs, various *Rana sp.* are found in forest and are also common. Among toads, *Bufo regularis*, although not confined to forest, is extremely common occurring in drier areas under leaves and fallen logs. Reptiles are represented by the **monitor lizard** *Varanus niloticus*, the common **hinged tortoise** *Kinixys crosa*, and some snakes, the largest of which, the **Gaboon viper** *Bitis gabonica*, is very poisonous, as is the **black cobra** *Naja melanoleuca*, another forest ground dweller.

A few birds feed almost exclusively on the forest floor and also build their nests on the ground, though of course they may take refuge by flying up into the trees in moments of danger. Notable examples are the **Crested Guinea-fowl** *Guttera edouardi* and **Latham's Francolin** *Francolinus lathami*. Several species of thrush are also essentially birds of the forest floor since this is the source of their food, though their nests are found in the trees. A common example is the **Ground Thrush**, *Geokichla sp.*

The ground-dwelling forest mammals vary with the condition of the forest. This may be explained by considering the sequence in the re-development of destroyed forest and the way it is repopulated by mammals as the forest is re-established. In the earlier stages, when the new growth consists of thick shrubs and young trees, only small mammals, such as **rats, shrews, porcupines,** and **squirrels,** which can penetrate the thick bush, are found. As time goes on the trees begin to form a closed canopy thus cutting off sunlight from the undergrowth, which consequently becomes thinner enabling larger running mammals such as the **duikers** *Cephalophus*, and *Philantomba*, the **water-chevrotain** *Hyemoschus aquaticus*, the **bush buck,** or **harnessed antelope** *Tragelophus scriptus*, and the antelope *Neotragus pygmaeus* to enter. At this stage a few carnivorous mammals such as the ***African civet*** *Viverra civetta* also appear.

As the tree canopy develops more storeys, the forest floor becomes more sparsely covered and more accessible to larger mammals, such as the **giant forest hog** *Pomatochoerus sp.*, a member of the pig family, and the **pygmy hippo** *Choeropsis liberiensis*, which, unlike its larger relation *Hippopotamus amphibious*, is more an inhabitant of marshy forest than water.

The list of forest ground-dwellers would be incomplete without a mention of the largest of all, the forest elephant *Loxodonta cyclotis*. It is not so commonly seen as the savanna elephants, but a poster bearing the inscription 'Elephant Pass' on the Ibadan–Benin road in Nigeria always reminds me of the presence of these animals in high forest, and reports of farms destroyed by elephants are a less pleasant reminder of these massive creatures.

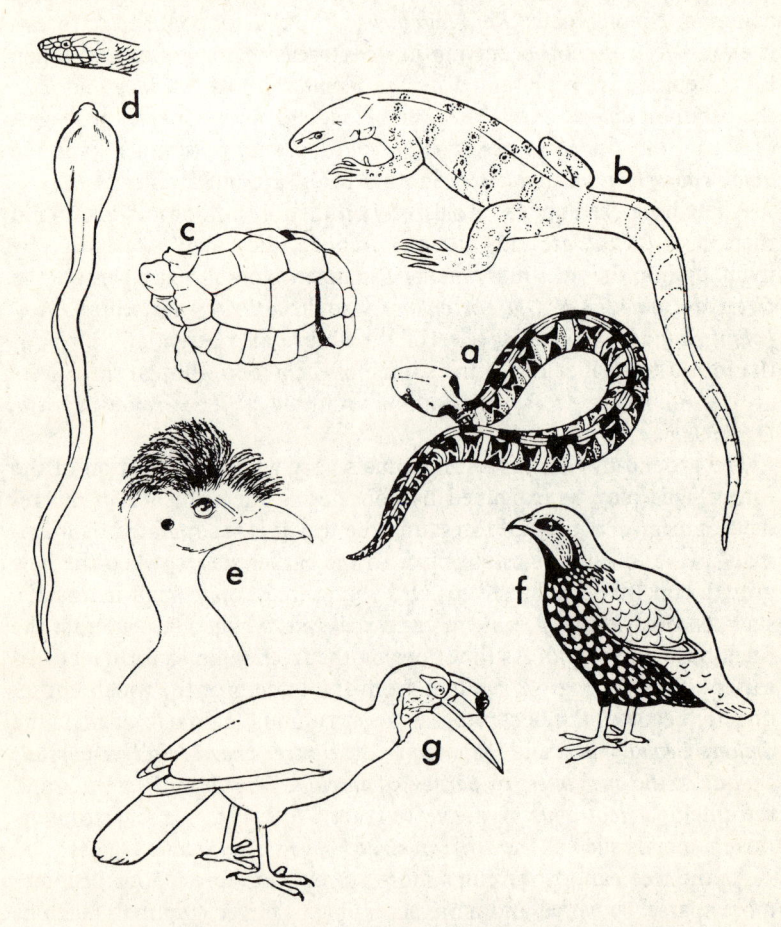

Fig. 61. Some forest ground-dwelling amphibia, reptiles, and birds.

(a) *Bitis gabonica* (gaboon viper)
(b) *Varanus niloticus* (monitor lizard)
(c) *Kinixys crosa* (common hinged tortoise)
(d) *Naja melanoleuca* (black cobra)
(e) *Guttera edouardi* (crested guineafowl)
(f) *Francolinus lathami* (Latham's Francolin)
(g) *Bucorvus abyssinicus* (ground hornbill)

Fig. 62. Some forest ground-dwelling mammals.

(a) *Crocidura poensis* (lesser musk shrew)
(b) *Atherurus africana* (brush tailed porcupine)
(c) *Philantomba maxwelli* (the maxwell's duiker)
(d) *Hyemoschus aquaticus* (the water chevrotain)
(e) *Viverra civetta* (the African civet)

Forest arboreal fauna

The majority of animals of high forest are arboreal. Dealing first with the invertebrates, the *Lepidoptera* and *Orthoptera* whose larvae have an essentially vegetable diet are the most numerous. Ants are, however, also plentiful, and the **tailor ants** represented by the common *Oecophylla longinoda* may be mentioned. These make their nests by drawing together the leaves with a sticky secretion, produced by their larvae, which the workers carry about and use as tubes of glue! This is one of the few cases of animals using their young as instruments, and may well be a matter for the Society for the Prevention of Cruelty to Children to investigate! Tree dwelling ants and termites also occur, building their 'carton' nests on branches or under the surface of leaves. The arachnida are well represented by a variety of **spiders,** and the annelida by **leeches.**

Among the vertebrates a number of interesting adaptations for arboreal life are found. The use of **claws** for holding on is found among lizards and carnivorous mammals. **Adhesive discs and ridges** are found

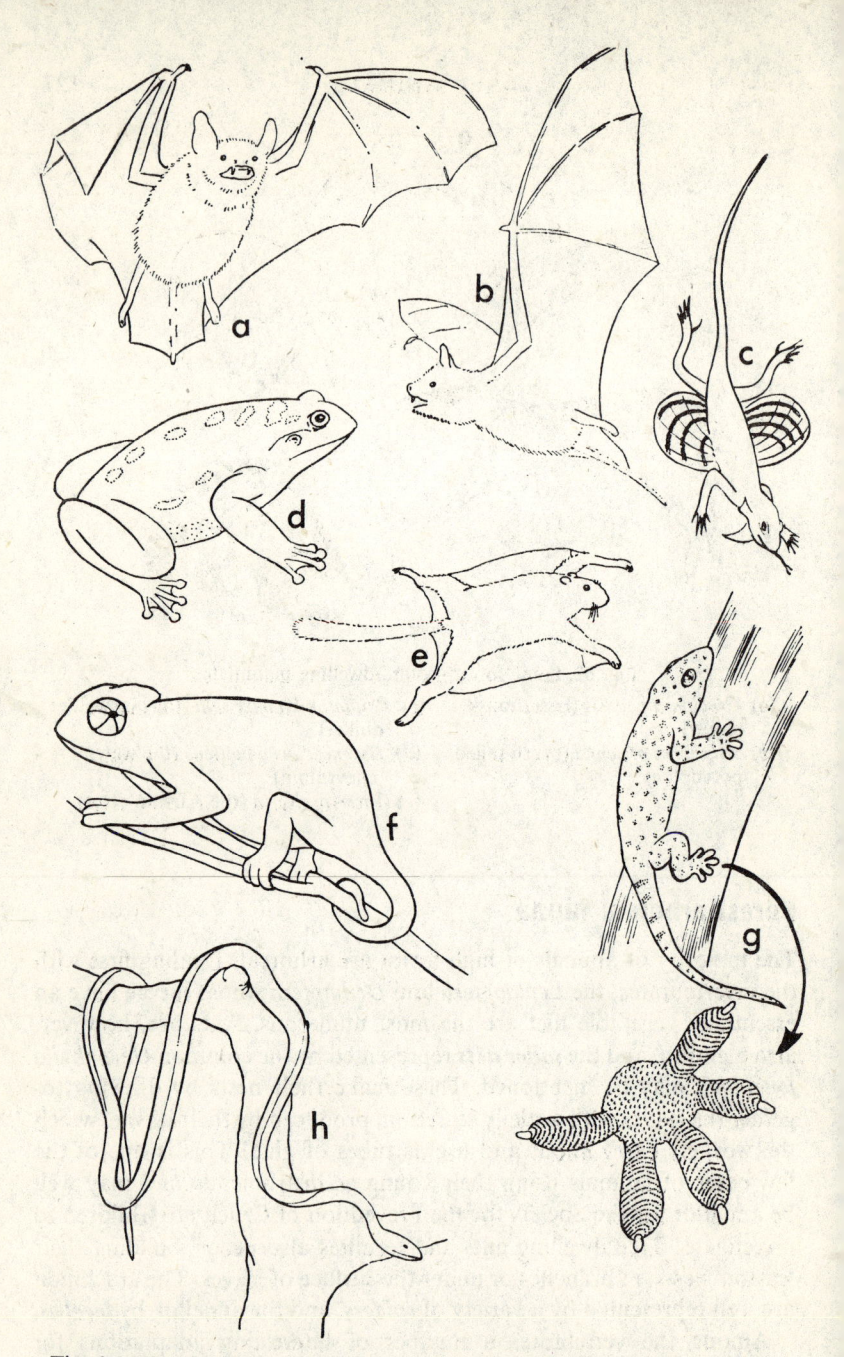

Fig. 63. Adaptations for arboreal life and flying in vertebrates other than birds.
(a) Wing of fruit bat
(b) Wing of insectivorous bat
(c) Expanded ribs in gliding lizard
(d) Webbed feet in gliding tree frog
(e) Expanded membrane in flying squirrel
(f) Prehensile tail and opposable digits in chameleon
(g) Adhesive discs on palms of gecko
(h) Elongation and winding habit in snake

LAND ANIMALS 129

on the toes of tree frogs, geckos, and hyraxes. There is also the development of **opposable digits** in both primates and chameleons, and the development of a **prehensile tail** in tree pangolins and chameleons. Finally **elongation of the body** enables some to wind round tree trunks

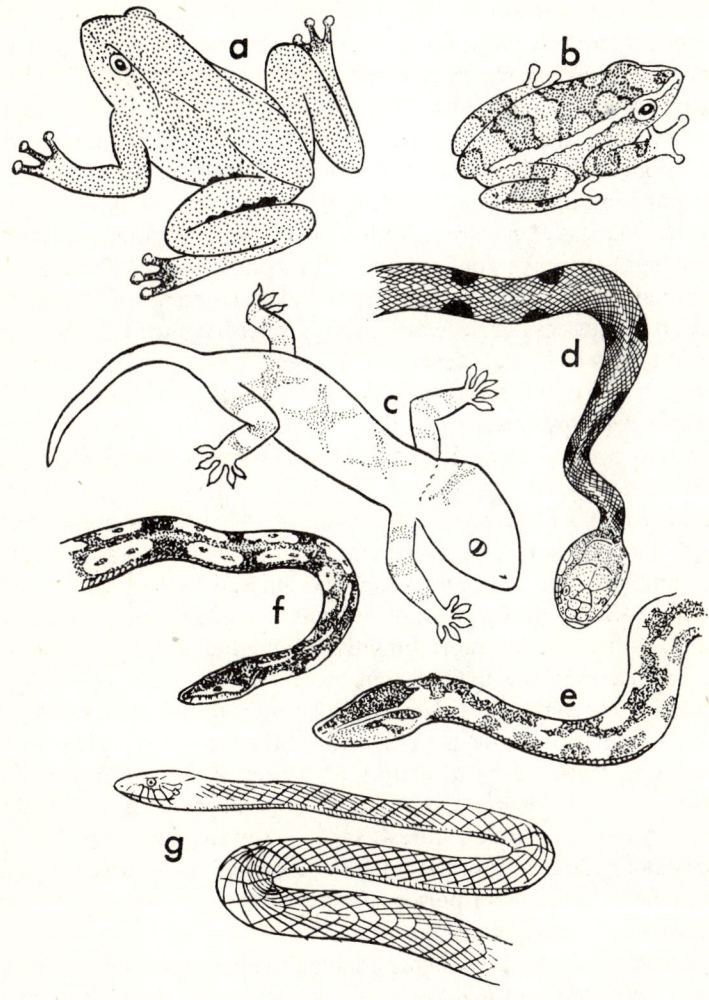

Fig. 64. Some common forest arboreal amphibians and reptiles.

(a) *Hyperolius fusciventris*
(b) *Hyperolius picturatus* } tree frogs
(c) *Hemidactylus brookii* (Brook's gecko)
(d) *Boiga blandingii* (Blanding's tree snake)
(e) *Python sabae* (African python)
(f) *Python regius* (royal python)
(g) *Dendroapsis viridis* (green mamba)

and branches as in such snakes as the **green mamba**. Adaptations for arboreal life are to be found in bats and flying squirrels, where a membrane is used for flying and gliding respectively. There are also some amphibia of the family *Rhacophoridae* in which the extensive webbing of the toes makes gliding possible.

Among the arboreal amphibia of the family *Rhacophoridae*, three genera, *Hyperolius*, *Afrixalus*, and *Leptolepis*, may be mentioned. The species of *Hyperolius* occur in a variety of gay colours. They lay their eggs on vegetation above water, wrapping them round stems and leaves. After hatching, the tadpoles wriggle into the water. *H. fusciventris* with a bright green dorsal coloration and chalk-white underside is by far the most common in forest, although it spreads to riverine forests of the savanna, whereas *H. picturatus* with brown dorsal coloration and yellow dorsolateral stripes is confined to high forest. *Afrixalus dorsalis* with black and white colour patterns is the most common of the second genus. It lays its eggs on vegetation above water but glues them together by slime in which they develop. The third genus is represented by *Leptolepis anbryi*, a forest form which lays its eggs on the ground where the larva develops in wet soil.

Reptiles are represented by the common gecko *Hemidactylus sp.*, which, although now common in houses, was originally tree dwelling. There are also a great variety of snakes, of which the pythons are the largest and probably best known though not confined to forest. The two common types, *Python sabae*, the **African python**, and *Python regius*, the **royal python,** are not difficult to differentiate because the latter is rather smaller, more brightly coloured, and ends in a curved tail. Smaller than the pythons but more typically forest dwelling is **Blanding's tree snake** *Boiga blandingii*. They occur in brown and black forms, and apart from the pythons and cobras are the only other forest snakes that reach a length of up to 2 metres. They are only slightly poisonous and belong to the group of back-fanged snakes, the *Colubridae*. Another common forest snake easy to identify by its red stripes along the length of the body is the **red-lined snake** *Botheopthalmus lineatus*, and among poisonous snakes the **green mamba** *Dendroapsis viridis* is typically arboreal.

There are many birds so highly adapted to life in the forest trees that despite their powers of flight they seldom leave this habitat. Prominent amongst these are the **Touracos,** several species of **hornbills** and the **Grey Parrot** *Psittacus erithacus*. These all feed on the fruits of the forest trees and make their nest in holes in these same trees. In the hornbills the males incarcerate the females by walling up the entrance to the nest with a mixture of dung and debris, but leaving a narrow slit through which the female and the young can be fed. Notable small birds of the forest are the many species of **bulbul** with a mixed diet of fruits and insects, while *shrikes, flycatchers,* and *drongos* feast on the rich insect life of the tropical forest. Bird predators of the forest include the **Goshawk** *Accipiter macroscelides* hunting by day and the **Wood-owl** *Strix woodfordi* hunting by night. Another characteristic group are the many species of *barbet* that not only feed on the fruits of the forest trees but also excavate their own nesting holes in the dead trees by using their particularly powerful beak for this purpose. One common species, the **Naked-faced Barbet** *Gymnobucco calvus*, nests in large colonies, so that it is not uncommon to find as many as a hundred nest holes in a single

Fig. 65. Some forest birds.

(a) *Lophoceros semifasciatus* (Allied Hornbill)
(b) *Vinago australis* (Green Fruit Pigeon)
(c) *Turacus persa* (West African Touraco)
(d) *Psittacus erithacus* (African Grey Parrot)
(e) *Accipiter macroscelids* (West African Goshawk)
(f) *Strix woodfordi* (Wood-owl)

dead tree. Closely related to the barbets are the **woodpeckers** adapted to locate and probe for beetle larvae as their source of food. A common forest woodpecker is the Fire-bellied *Mesopicos pyrrhogaster*. In conclusion it is worth mentioning that almost no migrant species of birds from Europe are able to utilize the high forest as a habitat during their stay in Africa.

We now proceed to the mammals of which the bats, because of their ability to fly, are rather widespread in distribution. ***Franquet's fruit bat*** *Epomophorus franquetti* is a well-known forest species, although difficult to differentiate from its close relation, the **Gambian fruit bat** *Epomophorus gambianus*, which is found both in forest and savanna. Another forest fruit bat which is easily identified is the **hammer-headed** bat, appropriately called *Hypsignathus monstrosus*. Insect-eating bats are numerous but not very well known because of their nocturnal activity. They are smaller than the fruit eaters and have comparatively larger ears, and their tails are connected with their legs by a membrane which helps them in flight. The commonest are the **slit-faced bats** of the genus *Nycteris* which shelter by day in hollow trees. The commonest of the group *Nycteris hispida* has a distribution throughout the forest and savanna living in man-made dark areas such as under culverts and bridges. However, two other species *N. arge* and *N. nana* have a more strictly forest distribution.

The lower primates include **Bosman's potto** *Perodicticus potto* and **Demidov's galago** or **bush baby** *Galagoides demidovii*. Both are nocturnal in habit sleeping for most of the day in the trees. Monkeys are abundant, and chief among them are the **black colobus monkey** *Colobus polykomos*, the **Diana monkey** *Cercopithecus diana*, the **mona monkey** *C. mona*, and the **mangabey monkey** *Cercocebus torquatus*. Even among this small group each shows a preference for a particular level within the forest at which it lives. The first are found in the uppermost storey and are capable of leaping long distances from one large tree to another; whilst the last live in the lowest storeys and even spend some time on the ground. The **drill** *Mandrillus leucophaeus* and the apes are primarily arboreal but have become secondarily ground dwellers, nevertheless they should be included in this list. Only a short tail remains in the mandrill, but the apes, including the **chimpanzee** *Pan troglodytes* and the **gorilla** *Gorilla gorilla* have lost their tails altogether. They walk on all fours, using the side of their feet and knuckles rather than their palms. Chimpanzees are very restricted in distribution in Nigeria, occurring only to the east of the Cross river and in the high forests of Sierra Leone and Liberia.

LAND ANIMALS 133

Fig. 66. Some common arboreal forest mammals (Primates).

(a) *Perodicticus potto* (Bosman's potto)
(b) *Galagoides demidovii* (bush baby)
(c) *Colobus polykomos* (colobus monkey)
(d) *Cercopithecus mona* (mona monkey)
(e) *Cercocebus torquatus* (mangabey monkey)
(f) *Mandrillus leucophaeus* (mandrill)
(g) *Pan troglodytes* (chimpanzee)

The ant eaters are represented by the **common pangolin Manis tricuspis** which has a prehensile tail unlike its ground-dwelling companion *M. gigantea*. Rodents include the flying squirrels represented by **Beecroft's flying squirrel Anomalurus beecrofti** and the **Niger flying squirrel *A. fraseri***.

There are a variety of normal squirrels, among which the **giant squirrel Protoxerus strangeri**, and the small **sun squirrel Heliosciurus punctatus** may be mentioned. Rats and mice have a wide distribution in both forest and savanna, some living in trees and others on the ground. Of the arboreal, the jumping mouse *Rattus morio* is a common forest type.

Carnivores are poorly represented in high forest when compared with savanna. They are represented by a few animals such as the **spotted**

palm civet *Nandinia binotata*, the **genet cats** *Genetta maculata* and *G. servalina*, and the **common mongoose** *Crossarchus obscurus*. The only large carnivore whose distribution extends from savanna into forest is the **leopard** *Panthera pardus*.

It only remains to mention the **tree hyrax** *Dendohyrax dorsalis*, whose special adaptation for arboreal life, namely the presence of suctorial discs on the feet, has been previously mentioned.

Fig. 67. More arboreal forest mammals.

(a) *Manis tricuspis* (common ant eater)
(b) *Protoxerus strangeri* (giant squirrel)
(c) *Heliosciurus punctatus* (sun squirrel)
(d) *Rattus morio* (jumping mouse)
(e) *Nandinia binotata* (spotted palm civet)
(f) *Genetta maculata* (genet cat)
(g) *Crossarchus obscurus* (mongoose)
(h) *Panthera pardus* (leopard)
(i) *Dendrohyrax dorsalis* (tree hyrax)

The savanna animals

Apart from the relatively narrow forest belt, which at its widest is less than 320 km, the rest of West Africa is covered by savanna grassland. It is believed, however, that the forest belt at an earlier period must have extended much further inland. The 'trade-mark' of savanna is the predominance of grass, but the range of plants composing it varies with the type of savanna area being considered.

The savanna is usually divided into a number of distinct sub-zones which run more or less parallel to the lines of latitude except for the sharp dip towards the coast in the Dahomey Gap previously mentioned in this chapter. These are the **Guinea** (sometimes divided further into southern and northern Guinea), **Sudan,** and **Sahel** sub-zones.

In the Guinea, which is the most extensive of the three, the grass is tall and thick, whereas in the Sahel it is scanty. In between the two extremes is the Sudan condition. The division into sub-zones is not vague or arbitrary, as there are plants which distinguish them fairly clearly, for example, species such as *Afzelia africana* (mahogany bean), *Butyrospermum paradoxum* (shea butter), and *Daniellia oliveri* (African balsam) are typical of the southern Guinea, whilst *Isoberlinia doka* is typical of northern Guinea.

The Sudan savanna is less woody than the Guinea and its vegetation of relatively short trees consists mainly of **acacias.** The date palm is also typical. In the Sahel, we have a very dry type of savanna tending towards sub-desert conditions. The trees are few and short, tending to be thorny, and the soil is usually sandy.

When considering the savanna, it is important to remember one important factor, namely, the activity of man in the annual burning of the grass during the dry season. A few natural fires may occur, but man burns it for game and for the provision of early grass. Although fire may stimulate the renewed growth of many savanna species, it severely damages many woody plants. Severe burning undoubtedly destroys many soil animals such as earthworms, and other larger animals which are killed if they are unable to escape.

In the savanna, conditions are ideal for grass eaters, runners, or hoppers of open grasslands as food is abundant, much more than on the forest floor and ground layers of forests. Large herbivores, mainly ungulates, and small rodents (rats, squirrels) and lagomorphs (hares) occur in great numbers and variety. A second group of animals typical of savanna are the carnivorous cats which prey on the herbivores and have developed stealth and a keen sense of smell to cope with the speed of their prey. Finally we have the scavengers, such as the hyenas, jackals, and vultures which clear up the carcases of dead animals.

Unlike the floral division into sub-zones, faunal divisions are much less obvious since the animals tend to be less restricted in distribution than the plants. Nevertheless, there are some species which are associated with specific floral sub-zones and are scarcely found in others. One example is the distribution of hares of the genus *Lepus* with three common species associated with the three savanna sub-zones. *Lepus zechi* is found to the south in Guinea savanna, the more northern Sudan zone has *L. canopus*, while still further north *L. chadensis* is found in Sahel savanna.

One last general remark about the savanna fauna is the higher incidence of **gregariousness** among its vertebrates than in forest animals, for example, baboons, antelopes, and elephants. Gregariousness is obviously advantageous to the group. Among those with a high level of social development, different members of the group may perform functions for the benefit of the whole group. Baboons for example have a sentry or sentries for the group which keep watch whilst others feed. Although similar advantage may not be immediately obvious in other groups with lower level of social development, there is experimental evidence to show that an individual is more easily preyed on when alone than when it is one of a group. In the exposed grasslands, gregariousness is an advantageous adaptation.

A brief mention of the invertebrate fauna of savanna must suffice because not very much is known at present, except that certain groups, namely, **earthworms, spiders, scorpions, collembola, grasshoppers, ants,** and **termites** are the most important. It is also known that the numbers of individuals and species vary with the dry and rainy seasons. In the rainy season, the smaller animals such as **collembola, ants, earwigs,** and **small beetles** are predominant, but in the dry season, the larger acridid **orthoptera, mantids,** and **crickets** are more common.

Termites deserve some special mention, as some species from forest and savanna have already been mentioned earlier in this chapter. Typical of savanna distribution are the **snouted harvester termites** *Trinervitermes* which are most abundant in this biome. Their mounds are small but occur in large numbers. They are all grass eaters, and workers collect food at night and plug the exits after the night's work. The jaws of the soldiers are greatly reduced and they rely on **chemical warfare** for the defence of their colony. Their swollen head contains a large gland in which a colourless irritant fluid is produced; this is squirted at the enemy as a sticky thread from the pore at the end of the snout. An interesting behavioural adaptation for life in savanna is their habit of moving into underground galleries during the dry season thereby avoiding the dangers of being burnt during grass fires.

A good example of savanna frog is *Rana galamensis*, and *Bufo regularis* with its wide distribution still represents the toads. Reptiles consist of a variety of **lizards, geckos, chameleons, skinks, tortoises,** and **snakes,** many of which are represented by species different from those of the forest. The poisonous grass snakes include the **spitting cobra** *Naja nigricollis*, the **night adder** *Causus rhombeatus*, and the **puff adder** *Bitis arietans*. Among non-poisonous forms, the pythons are common, and a variety of smaller savanna snakes are also found. In sandy areas of Sahel savanna the **Rufous beaked snake** *Rhamphiophis oxyrhynchus* and the **sand boa** *Eryx muelleri*, which are both well adapted for life in sand, possessing a wedge-shaped snout for digging into the sand during the day are typical.

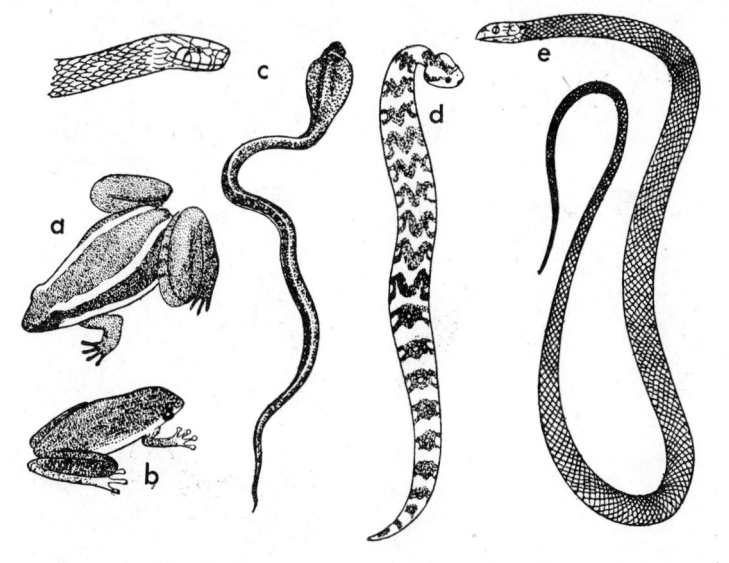

Fig. 68. Some savanna amphibia and reptiles.

(a) *Rana galamensis* (savanna frog)
(b) *Hyperolius nitidulus* (savanna tree frog)
(c) *Naja nigricollis* (spitting cobra)
(d) *Bitis arietans* (puff adder)
(e) *Rhamphiophis oxyrhynchus* (beaked snake)

The birds of savanna include many seed eaters, but insect eaters are also plentiful. As previously mentioned, savanna birds are better known than those confined to forest, and quite often a list of common birds is really a list of savanna types. A number of birds which may be observed in open grassland are shown in Fig. 69.

Not all these birds are restricted to savanna; in fact some southward migration during the dry season is to be expected. They also frequent areas of derived savanna in the forest zone, farmland, and around human habitation. Three birds to be found in West Africa in both

Fig. 69. Common birds of savanna and open areas.

(a) *Lophoceros nasutus* (Grey Horn Bill)
(b) *Bubulcus ibis* (cattle egret)
(c) *Necrosyrtes monarchus* (common vulture)
(d) *Milvus migrans* (West African black kite)
(e) *Accipiter badius* (shikra)
(f) *Francolinus bicalcaratus* (common bush fowl)
(g) *Columba guinea* (speckled pigeon)
(h) *Ptilopsis leucotis* (white-faced owl)
(i) *Centropos senegalensis* (senegal coucal)
(j) *Mesopicos goertae* (grey-headed woodpecker)
(k) *Corvus albus* (pied crow)

Fig. 69 *continued*

(*l*) *Quelea quelea* (dioch)
(*m*) *Balearica pavonina* (West African crowned crane)
(*n*) *Poicephalus senegalus* (Senegal parrot)
(*o*) *Uraeginthus bengalus* (cordon bleu)
(*p*) *Lagonosticta senegalensis* (fire finch)
(*q*) *Spermestes cucullatus* (bronze manikin)
(*r*) *Serinus mozambicus* (yellow-fronted canary)
(*s*) *Motacilla aguimp* (common wagtail)
(*t*) *Pycnonotus barbatus* (bulbul)
(*u*) *Plesiositagra cucullatus* (village weaver)

savanna and forest are the **common wagtail** *Motacilla aguimp*, the **village weaver** *Plesiositagra cucullatus*, and the **bulbul** *Pycnonotus barbatus*. The last is very common around villages and farms, and the weaver commonly nests on palm trees especially in the forest zone.

Two large birds, the **ostrich** *Struthio camelus*, the largest of living birds, is found mostly in Sahel savanna and is entirely ground dwelling, and the **marabou stork** *Leptoptilos crumeniferus*, which flies well, is found mostly in northern Guinea and Sudan savanna, where it is essentially a scavenger.

The mammals have already been stated as forming a conspicuous part of the savanna fauna. (In the following description, a number of back references will be made to forest species to give a better comparative picture of mammalian distribution.) Beginning with the shrews and hedge-hogs (Insectivora), the **West African hedge-hog** *Erinaceus albiventris* is confined to savanna; shrews of the genus *Crocidura*, however, show a more interesting distribution. **Mann's shrew** *Crocidura manni* is distributed both in forest and savanna zones, *C. giffardi* is confined to Guinea and Sudan savanna, *C. foxi* is confined to Guinea, *C. arethusa* to Sudan, and *C. diana* to Sahel savanna.

Among the fruit bats the **straw-coloured fruit bat** *Eidolon helvum* is found in all areas, but bats of the genus *Epomophorus* which are very

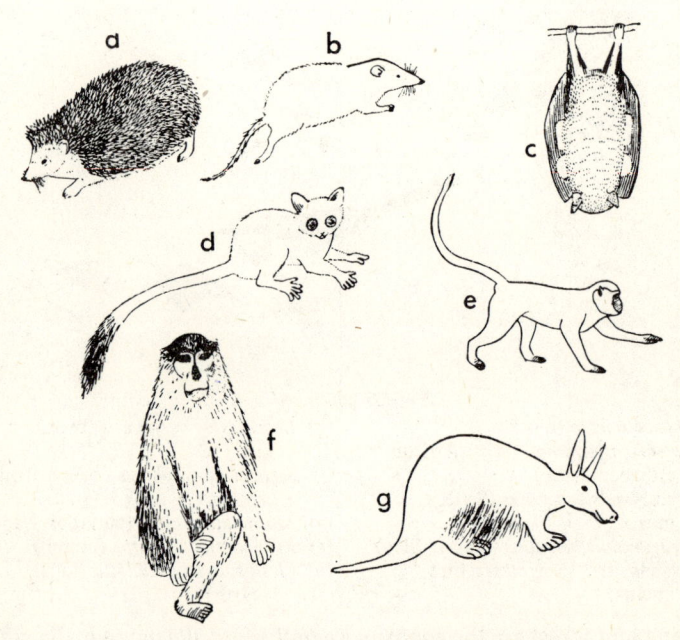

Fig. 70. Some mammals of savanna grassland.

(a) *Erinaceus albiventris* (West African hedge-hog)
(b) *Crocidura giffardi* (Giffard's shrew)
(c) *Epomophorus anurus* (savanna fruit bat)
(d) *Galago senegalensis* (senegal galago)
(e) *Cercopithecus aethiops* (green monkey)
(f) *Erythrocebus patas* (patas monkey)
(g) *Orycteropus afer* (aard vark)

common have a more interesting distribution. *E. franqueti* has been mentioned as a forest and savanna species. *E. anurus* is found in all savanna belts whilst *E. pusillus* is restricted to Guinea savanna. Among the insect-eating bats, represented by members of the genus *Nycteris*,

LAND ANIMALS 141

we also find a similar distribution. *N. hispida* is appropriately called the common slit-faced bat and is found in all savanna areas. *N. macrotis* is confined to Guinea savanna whilst *N. thebaica* is found in both Guinea and Sudan savanna.

The **giant pangolin** *M. gigantea* is a savanna form. Unlike the other pangolin of the forest, it is a ground dweller. Its tail is not prehensile and is only used as an extra prop for support. Another ant eater, although not belonging to the same order of mammals as the pangolin, is the **aard vark** *Orycteropus afer* found in all savanna areas.

Hares of the genus *Lepus*, whose distribution has already been mentioned, are typical savanna animals. Although squirrels have a pre-

Fig. 71. Some savanna rodents.

(a) *Lepus canopus* (northern hare)
(b) *Heliosciurus gambianus* (savanna tree squirrel)
(c) *Xerus erythropus* (red-legged ground squirrel)
(d) *Lemniscomys striatus* (spotted grass rat)
(e) *Hystrix cristata* (crested porcupine)
(f) *Thryonomys swinderianus* (cutting grass)

dominantly forest distribution, they are represented in savanna by the savanna tree squirrel *Heliosciurus gambianus* of the Guinea savanna, the red-legged ground squirrel *Xerus erythropos* found in both Guinea and Sudan savannas and the Chad ground squirrel *Xerus chadensis* of Sahel savanna. **Rats, mice,** and **porcupines** have a predominantly savanna distribution, living among the grass (although some climb into the trees)

142 ANIMAL SPECIES ECOLOGY

Fig. 72. Some carnivores and ungulates of the savanna.

(a) *Felis caracal* (desert lynx)
(b) *Hyena striata* (striped hyena)
(c) *Crocuta crocuta* (spotted hyena)
(d) *Lycaon pictus* (hunting dog)
(e) *Acynonyx jubatus* (cheetah)
(f) *Phacochoerus aethiopicus* (wart-hog)
(g) *Sylvicapra grimmi* (crowned duiker)
(h) *Syncerus nanus* (bush cow)
(i) *Tragelaphus scriptus* (harnessed antelope)
(j) *Gazella rufifrons* (red-fronted gazelle)

and digging tunnels in the ground. The giant rat *Cricetomys gambianus*, already mentioned as an important member of the forest fauna, spreads into savanna, and other rats include the **spotted grass rat** *Lemniscomys striatus* and the **multimamate rat** *Rattus natalensis*. Among the porcupines, the **large-crested porcupine** *Hystrix cristata*, and the small *H. aerula* are found in different savanna areas, the first in Guinea and Sudan, and the latter in Sahel. The **cutting grass** *Thryonomys swinderianus* is a savanna form although in recent times it has found its way into forest.

Carnivores are another predominant savanna group. In the forest, apart from the civets, genets, and mongooses, the only large carnivore *Panthera pardus leopardus* is in fact a race of the savanna species *Panthera pardus*. Other true cats (*felidae*), including the **lion** *Panthera leo*, the **cheetah** *Acynonyx jubatus*, the caracal or desert lynx *Felix caracal*, and the **wild cat** *Felix lybica*, have an entirely savanna distribution. Of the scavenging hyenas, the **spotted hyena** *Crocuta crocuta* has a distribution in both Guinea and Sudan savannas, while the **striped hyena** *Hyena hyena* is found only in Sahel. The foxes and jackals (*canidae*) also have a savanna distribution especially in Sudan and Sahel, the **hunting dog** *Lycaon pictus* being a notable example.

Mention must be made of the **savanna elephant** *Loxodonta africana*, with a distribution in Guinea, Sudan, and part of the Sahel savanna before going on to the true hoofed mammals which are the best adapted animals for life in the savanna grasslands. The odd-toed ungulates are represented by the **black rhinoceros** *Diceros bicornis* now confined to a small area of Sudan savanna. Both the **horse** *Equus cabalus* and the **camel** *Camelus sp.*, which also really belong to this group, do not occur in the wild state, but are domesticated animals well suited to life in the savanna.

The even-toed ungulates include members of the pig family represented in savanna by the **wart-hog** *Phacochoerus aethiopicus* a close relation to the river hog previously mentioned as having a forest distribution. The **Nubian giraffe** *Giraffa camelopardalis* is rare in Sudan savanna, and finally the antelope group is represented by a great variety of animals. Although duikers have been mentioned as typical of forest, **Grimm's duiker** or crowned **duiker** *Sylvicapra grimmi* has a savanna distribution. Other even-toed ungulates which are widespread in savanna include the **West African buffalo** or **bush cow** *Syncerus nanus*, the **reedbuck** *Redunca nigeriensis*, the **oribi** *Ourebia ourebi*, the **gazelle** *Gazella rufifrons*, and, although it is found in forest, the common bush buck or **harnessed antelope** *Tragelaphus scriptus*.

Desert fauna

Although true desert areas are really outside West Africa proper, it is necessary to make some mention of desert fauna for the sake of completeness. One of the chief problems of land life is water conservation, but in the desert, with its almost complete lack of water, this problem is all the more magnified. The fact that some animals have become adapted to life in desert at all is an indication of the very high adaptive capability of living organisms.

Of the world's deserts, the Sahara is the largest with an estimated area of about 7 million square kilometres. In the stringent conditions of very low rainfall, low humidity, excessive diurnal and seasonal variation in temperature, intense and prolonged radiation, and the violent winds obtaining in deserts, rarity of flora and fauna is to be expected. Furthermore, relatively few species have undergone specialized adaptation to enable them to survive under these rigorous conditions; some of these adaptations are given below.

(a) *Development of integument.* In insects, an excessively wax-proofed integument is developed which remains impermeable to water even at high temperatures. This feature is also adopted by many reptiles.

(b) *Burrowing.* Humidity is higher within the soil than in the atmosphere, so water loss is reduced by burrowing. Snout and feet are often appropriately modified, as in the desert toad.

(c) *Nocturnal habit* is adopted by most desert animals. Temperature is lower and humidity higher at night than by day and there is even the possibility of dew formation which desert animals can utilize.

(d) *Use of metabolic water* is shown by all forms but especially by many tenebrionid beetles. Also, rodents of the family *Hetromyidae* can live on dry seed almost indefinitely.

(e) *Excretion and defaecation of dry matter* is common among many reptiles, in which uric acid and guanin, from which almost the last molecule of water has been reabsorbed is produced. The camel produces a very concentrated urine and dry faeces.

(f) *Ability to tolerate dehydration*—as in the camel, which can tolerate loss of 40% of its body fluids.

(g) *Diminished activity of sweat glands* for water economy is found in the camel.

(h) *Enlarged feet or fringed toes* for walking on loose sand, again seen in the camel.

Plate IX. Dog-faced baboon *Papio anubis*

Plate X. Rock fauna
(a) Rock hyrax *Procavia ruficeps*
(b) Fat-tailed gecko *Hemitheoconyx caudicinctus*

(i) **Elongated legs** for hopping or jumping, seen in the jerboas.
(j) **Sand-coloured body** for protection in almost all desert animals.

In spite of all these adaptations, nowhere is the dependence of animal life on vegetation more evident than in deserts; because the plants provide not only food but in many cases all the water too. The battle against drought is first won by the plants, and where they exist the animals follow. Succulent plants, chief among which are the cacti (of which there are over 1000 species) are the 'storage tanks' of the desert. Among desert animals are *antelopes, gazelles, jackals, foxes, jerboas, small rodents, reptiles, birds,* and many *small insects,* some of which require to drink only irregularly. For example, the camel will survive without water for about 7 days in summer and is capable of drinking 124 litres of water in a few minutes. Others obtain all their water from the food, herbivores from the cacti and carnivores from the body fluid of their prey. A third group depend on metabolic water and seem to be able to survive almost indefinitely on dry seeds and fruits; an indication of water conservation at its very best.

Montane fauna

The areas of montane vegetation in West Africa include those in the Cameroon Republic, Mali, and the Obudu Plateau of Eastern Nigeria. Vegetation which truly merits the designation of montane, which may be montane forest or montane grassland, occurs only above 1500 metres, although opinions differ on this, and no hard and fast height limit can be stated. Relatively little is known of the fauna of these areas except for its birds. One general feature is that when birds of the same species occur in the lower and higher altitudes of a mountain, the ones from the higher altitude, that is from the montane region, are usually darker coloured. Several groups of birds have their montane representatives, e.g. *wagtails* and *sunbirds.* The wagtails are waterside birds, and the *mountain wagtail Motacilla clara* is found along the rushing rocky streams of montane forest. It feeds on flies, dragon flies, and other riverine insects. The **Double-collared Sunbird** *Cinnyris reichenowi* is found in montane grassland, and like other sunbirds it thrives on nectar. A feature of the montane zone is the occurrence of abundant flowers most of the year, and it is therefore not surprising that sunbirds flourish and are represented in the montane zone by several distinct species.

Rock and cave fauna

There are a number of special areas usually inhabited by distinct animals irrespective of the surrounding vegetational zone. Rocky hills with their caves have a peculiar fauna of their own and belong to this category. Baboons (Plate IX) for instance are almost invariably found where there are rocks in the savanna, as also are the rock-hyrax or conie, *Procavia ruficeps*. Like their relation, the tree hyrax *Dendrohyrax* (whose feet are adapted for holding on to branches), the rock hyrax has its feet adapted for holding to the rock surface. *Procavia* is a small mammal, rather like a rodent, but zoologists agree that it is probably a close relation of the elephant, the resemblance to rodents being only superficial. A reptilian inhabitant of rocky areas is the fat tailed gecko *Hemitheconyx caudicinctus* (See Plate IX.)

Fig. 73. Montane birds.
(a) *Motacilla clara* (mountain wagtail)
(b) *Cinnyris reichenowi* (double-collared sunbird)

Bats are common inhabitants of caves. In spite of the darkness prevailing inside, they are able to find their way about. This is because they possess a *'radar' mechanism,* a system by which they produce sounds inaudible to the human ear which are reflected by obstacles, which they can thus detect and avoid. What better adaptation could an animal possess for living in darkness?

Nature conservation

It will be appropriate to conclude this chapter on the terrestrial fauna with a mention of the importance of nature conservation in West Africa. In this respect we are lagging behind the countries of East Africa where the creation of reserves is already beginning to have an impact on the life of the people, in particular, the younger generation.

What is meant by nature conservation? *It is simply the bringing of large areas of natural flora and fauna under thoughtful management and controlled utilization.*

Management is the key word here. In the keeping of poultry, cattle, and sheep, man has learnt that scientific management is essential. The same thoughtful management can be extended to wild life with equal success. This advocates a policy of *cropping the surplus,* whilst a *breeding stock* is carefully conserved. The concept that a conserved area should not be tapped at all is quite wrong. Trees may be felled, and animals may be culled, but this is done only after careful scientific planning. It is only by doing this that the fullest benefits from natural resources can be obtained. Perhaps in view of the often erroneous conception of conservation, *nature management* would be a more used term.

Sometimes, those who advocate nature conservation are accused of being sentimental and unrealistic. It is argued that since man's most urgent need is for food, and that he requires timber for shelter, it is inevitable that he cuts down and burns the forests to provide space for agriculture, and that the grazing of cattle in the grasslands must take precedence over any attempt at conservation. This is clearly a shortsighted policy, which does not take account of future generations who have a right to the gifts of nature as well as ourselves. Apart from this moral reason, there is an important ecological reason for conservation. There is no doubt that because of man's activities, the ecological balance is irreversibly upset and this will lead to disastrous consequences unless we do something about it; for example, what effect would it have if all vultures and hyenas were destroyed? How would their duties as scavengers be carried out? It is interesting to note that vultures are regarded in most societies as special birds, which must not be killed. The same protection has not been extended to the hyena. In a recent investigation of a newly created game reserve, it was found that the spotted hyena *Crocuta crocuta* was virtually non-existent. It was noted that in past years, a cash bounty had been paid by the local authority for every hyena skin! Conservation would attempt to re-establish the natural ecological balance in the given area.

A third reason for conservation is educational. It enables people to get to know animals and plants—perhaps it is this aspect that is regarded as sentimental, especially when tourists travel many thousands of miles to see wild life in another area. Nevertheless, this is a valid reason for conservation especially when the visitors do not come emptyhanded! In well-conserved areas, where wild life can be seen, visitors are attracted and a vigorous tourist trade can develop.

There are at present a number of forest and game reserves in West Africa mostly in savanna. One of the largest is the newly created **Yankari Game Reserve** in Bauchi Province of Northern Nigeria. It has an area of about 184 000 hectares of Guinea and Sudan savanna, and areas of riverine forest. There is a need for more such reserves, especially in forest areas, and active selection of areas with rare and interesting flora and fauna needs to be made as soon as possible. It is gratifying to note that Wild Life Advisory Committees have been set up in a number of West African countries to handle this problem.

Finally, there is a great need for the establishment of Biological Gardens which are easily accessible from the large towns. Some of the animals, especially the dangerous ones, will have to be caged, but it is desirable that as many kinds as possible should be enclosed in areas similar to their normal habitation but where they are more or less unrestricted. All these things will go a long way in the education of future generations of West Africans in matters pertaining to their fauna and flora.

Things to do

The land fauna is the most easily accessible for study. There should be no excuse therefore for not making a detailed study of a selected area. The following are suggested:

(i) *Insect collection.* Collect insects from *forest, riverine forest,* and *savanna.* Compare your collections. It is advisable that dry and rainy season collections should be made. For this exercise, a couple of nets for catching insects, and bottles with perforated covers are all that will be required.

(ii) *Collection of soil animals.* Mark out a small area of forest, farmland, or savanna about 10 cm by 10 cm, and 10 cm deep; and collect the soil. Extract the soil animals with a *Tullgren funnel* if available. If not available, place the soil in a vessel of warm water and stir. The animals will float on the surface of the water. This is called the flotation method. Compare the densities of fauna in selected areas.

(iii) *A collection of small vertebrates.* This could be undertaken at different times of the year in selected areas. Traps may be used for mammals. A piece of farmland left fallow can be studied over a number of years. In such a study it is advisable to make both floral and faunal observations.

(iv) *Visit a menagerie or game reserve.*

Part III: Population and community ecology

9: The interrelationships of animals

It has been previously explained that, apart from the effects of physical ecological factors on organisms, the different organisms themselves affect one another within a given population or community. First of all, it is important to define the use of the two words, **population** and **community**. *A population is a group of animals of the same or closely related species, whilst a community consists of all the different species within a particular area.* When considering relationships between organisms within a population, they are described as *intraspecific,* and within a community as *interspecific*. It will be remembered that in the first chapter reference was made to population and community ecology as branches of ecology. It is important to realize that most of the advances in ecological studies today are in these fields.

Population characteristics

Populations have certain characteristics which are distinctive, and which are not shared by individuals or by the community. These are, (*a*) **density**—or population size per unit space, (*b*) **birth rate**—the rate at which new individuals are added to the population, (*c*) **age distribution**—the proportion of individuals of different ages in the population, (*d*) **death rate**—the rate at which individuals are lost by death, (*e*) **dispersion**—the way in which individuals are distributed, and (*f*) **growth rate**—the net result of birth rate, death rate, and dispersion.

Density of population

Of these characteristics, density of a population is probably the most important factor which determines the degree of intraspecific relationships. For any population, there is an **optimum density** attainable under natural conditions. Sometimes this may be exceeded, become extremely high and become known as a **population irruption,** as for example during locust swarms. For most animals, there is a natural regulation in numbers, and it is only when the ecological balance is dislocated that we have an unusual increase or decrease in density.

The result of the hunting activity of man on some animals in West Africa is an example of unusual low density. The great apes in the forest zone and the lion in savanna have a very low density. On the other hand, there are times when some animals attain an abnormally high density which makes an organized hunt necessary. For example, the army has been called out in recent years to shoot baboons *Papio anubis*, in Northern Nigeria. We may also get an abnormally high density when an animal is tabooed, or when a new animal is introduced to an area where its natural enemies are absent.

Birth rate (natality)

When we think of birth rate, the natural tendency is to think of man, and his production of, usually, one offspring at a time. Among most animals, this is not the case, the average number of offspring being higher. Although most animals produce a large number of reproductive cells, there is very great disparity in the numbers of young eventually produced by different animals. Let us take as examples the toad *Bufo regularis* and the rainbow lizard *Agama agama*. Both may develop millions of reproductive cells, but *Bufo* will spawn to produce hundreds of eggs, whereas *Agama* will lay on the average only 5–6 eggs, and at most 8 eggs at one time. The eggs of *Bufo* hatch into the familiar tadpole, most of which are eaten by other animals in the community and only very few eventually metamorphose, find their way to land, and become part of the toad population. *Agama*, on the other hand, protects its few eggs by burying them in the soil. Here they develop and hatch as little lizards without the ordeal of a helpless larval stage. There is no doubt that the percentage of offspring actually resulting from the eggs laid in *Agama*, and consequently its birth rate, will be much higher than that in the toad.

These examples show that birth rate is linked intimately with the general life history of the animal. It is not being suggested that certain animals 'realize' that they have a vulnerable stage in their life history and therefore compensate by laying many eggs; rather, they are able to survive in spite of this vulnerable stage in their life history **because** they have an appropriate adaptation, namely **high fecundity**.

The extremes of birth rates are found in the higher mammals such as primates on the one hand, and parasitic animals on the other. Mammals produce very few offspring, but these are developed internally, and after birth are fed and defended by their parents for some time. Parasites, apart from their larval stages, have the problem of finding appropriate hosts, which in some may involve finding one or more intermediate hosts before returning to the primary host. With these hazards, it is only to be expected that, for parasites to survive, they must have a prodigious fecundity. It is estimated that a single tapeworm will produce several million eggs, but the chances of one of them reaching maturity, especially in surroundings where good sanitation obtains, are practically nil; and certainly far less than that of the single offspring of a typical mammal.

Age distribution and death rate

Within any population, we usually find a range of individuals of different ages and sizes. Although there is a maximum age attainable (at least the records for most species suggest there is), very few in fact reach

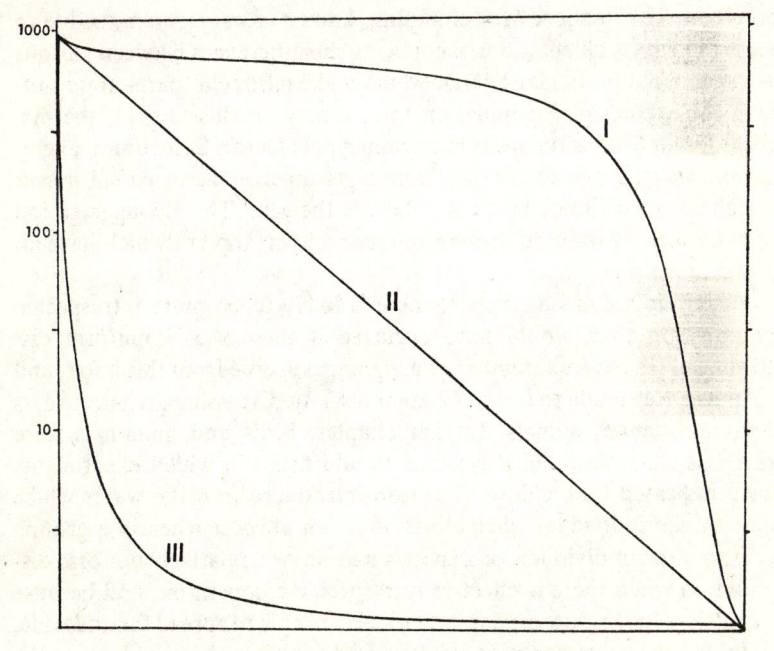

Fig. 74. Survivorship curves in animals.

that age. For biological purposes, information regarding age distribution and death rate is given in the form of *survivorship curves* (Fig. 74) which indicate the number of probable survivors within a given unit of the population. It is known that survivorship in most animal populations approximates to one of these curves. Curve I is known to apply to many birds and mammals, and indicates that many of the young survive, through parental care, and afterwards there is a gradual loss in numbers with age. Curve II applies, in varying forms, to animals in which parental care is at its highest; this includes man. Curve III applies to all those animals which have a larval stage in their life history, during which there is high mortality.

Population dispersion

It is well recognized that over any particular area dispersion of individuals is almost never uniform, but is very often patchy, individuals tending to occupy the most suitable areas. This is well shown in the distribution of planktonic organisms which occur in patches in the oceans of the world. Among land animals, patchy distribution is also common. This tendency for clumping, known as **aggregation,** is due to various factors, chief among them being the differences between various areas within a particular habitat which make particular parts more suitable for a particular population than others. In this respect, the distribution of food is the most important single factor. Sometimes, aggregation may be due to a reproductive get-together as in **palolo worms** which spawn on some particular days of the year. Thirdly, aggregation may be socially induced as in termites and hymenoptera which have an elaborate social system.

When individuals aggregate, there is likely to be more intraspecific competition than would have occurred if there was a uniform distribution. However, a number of advantages accrue from this habit, and reference was made to this in Chapter 8 whilst discussing gregariousness among savanna animals. In that chapter, birds and mammals were given as examples, and it remains to add fishes in which experiments have indicated that a dose of poison introduced into the water which may kill an individual when alone, may not affect it when in a group.

Less often, individuals of a species may show a relatively uniform distribution when there is effective intraspecific competition, and because of efficient locomotor organs individuals are able to spread far and wide.

By far the most common pattern of dispersion of individuals is the **clumped pattern,** but when groups are considered, the random pattern is more characteristic.

As for the methods of dispersing, there are three main methods, namely: by use of various locomotor organs (swimming, walking, flying); by drifting with currents of air or water; and by clinging to moving objects either of plant or animal origin.

Population growth

Population growth is the net product of three other characteristics; namely birth rate, death rate, and dispersion; and it is also closely related to density. Some populations tend to be self-limiting in that the rate of growth decreases as the density increases; such growth is said to be *density dependent*. There are others which tend to grow in geometric sequence and are not limited by density until some force outside the population (e.g. other populations) comes into play; such growth is said to be *density independent*.

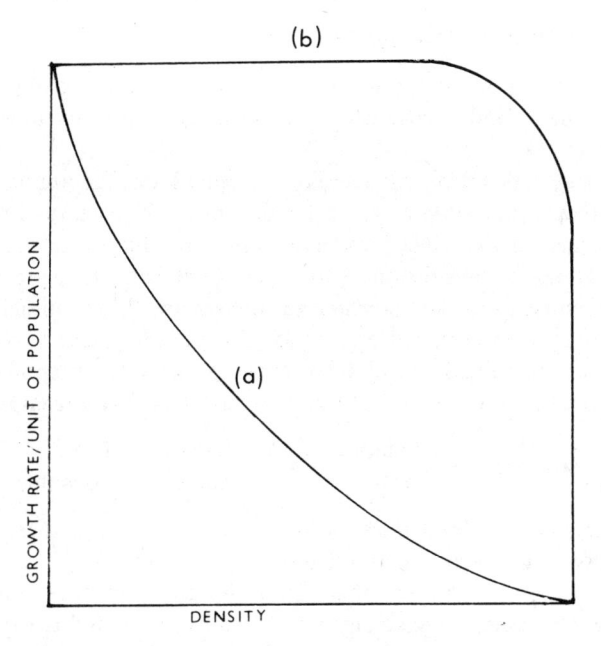

Fig. 75. Growth rates of populations.
(*a*) Density dependent
(*b*) Density independent

Competition

When two or more organisms utilize common resources which are not in adequate supply, competition ensues. When this is between organisms of the same species, it is described as *intraspecific competition,* and between organisms of different species as *interspecific competition*. Intraspecific competition is of particular importance in populations in which the growth rate is density dependent; as more individuals join the population, competition increases, and the rate of growth is bound to decrease.

It has been shown that even when common resources required by two or more organisms are not in short supply, there may still be competition since animals are sometimes known to harm each other as they seek their various needs; for example, the organisms might secrete substances which interfere with each other. This is sometimes called *mutual inhibition* and it is clearly a type of competition.

Community characteristics

All organisms in a community may be classed in three groups on the basis of their food relationship: (*a*) producers, (*b*) consumers, and (*c*) reducers.

The producers are the plants and phytoplankton; the animals which feed on them are *consumers*, and the reducers are the bacteria, fungi, and related organisms which act on the remains of producers and consumers, and return inorganic substances to the environment. There are different types of consumers. The *primary consumers* are those animals which feed directly on the producers, whilst the *secondary and tertiary consumers* are the animals which feed on the primary and secondary consumers respectively. These last two may also be called *predators*.

$$\text{Producer} \rightarrow \text{Primary Consumer} \rightarrow \text{Secondary Consumer} \rightarrow \text{Tertiary Consumer}$$

It is this type of food relationships that is called a *food chain*; in it there may be between one and five links.

Let us consider some examples from the areas we have studied. In the intertidal zone, we have algae on the substratum and pytoplankton in the water as producers. Feeding on the algae are the limpets such as *Siphonaria* and *Fissurella*, and on the plankton, barnacles such as *Balanus* and *Chthamalus*. Feeding on these are the carnivorous molluscs such as *Thais*. The remains of all these may be consumed by the scavenging hermit crab. In the open sea and in freshwater we have the types of food chain shown diagrammatically in Fig. 76.

The food relationships of animals are not quite as straightforward as food chains seem to imply. Although a consumer may have a favourite food, it may feed on others as well. Furthermore it may change its diet as it grows, whilst it is in turn preyed on by different animals as it becomes larger. In view of this interwoven nature of the food relationships

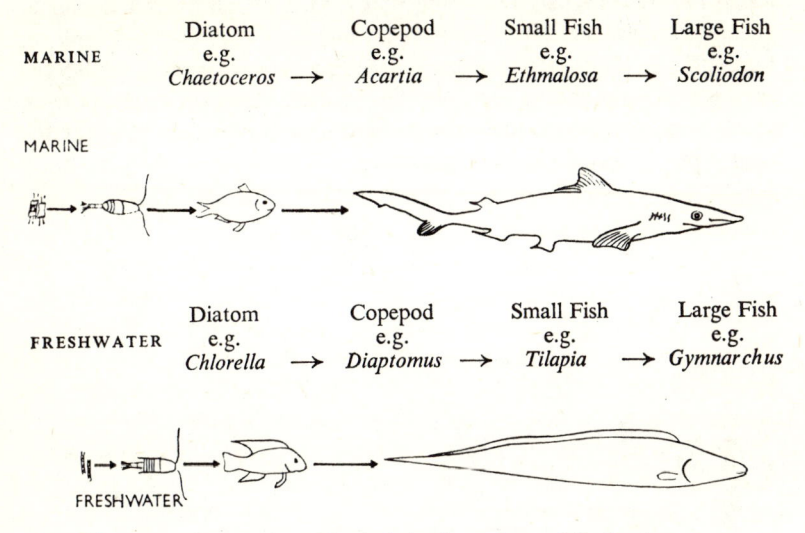

	Diatom e.g. Chaetoceros	→	Copepod e.g. Acartia	→	Small Fish e.g. Ethmalosa	→	Large Fish e.g. Scoliodon
MARINE							

	Diatom e.g. Chlorella	→	Copepod e.g. Diaptomus	→	Small Fish e.g. Tilapia	→	Large Fish e.g. Gymnarchus
FRESHWATER							

Fig. 76. Examples of food chains in marine and freshwater.

of organisms, the term *food web* is now considered more appropriate. An interesting exercise would be to work out the food web of a particular local community. Another interesting feature of food relationships is the tendency to have the largest number and bulk of small-sized producers being fed on by fewer numbers but larger-sized consumers. This is shown diagrammatically in Fig. 77 in the form of a *pyramid of numbers* depicting the increase in size and decrease in numbers from the base to the top of the pyramid. We know from everyday experience that not all food chains follow this pattern. Many large animals feed on microscopic organisms, thus *breaking the chain;* for example, the largest animals in the world today, the whale-bone whales, do just this by filtering plankton in the sea, and the largest dinosaurs of the age of reptiles are known to have been herbivorous. Elephants, giraffes, horses, and related forms are all herbivorous. In a long chain, food energy is lost in each transfer from producer to the different grades of consumers; so that an animal which feeds directly on the producer is at some advantage from the energy point of view.

One final type of food relationship is that between phyto- and zooplankton. It is known that high density of phyto- and zooplankton do not usually occur at one point at the same time, but the phytoplankton maximum usually precedes that of the zooplankton. This is known as an *inverse relationship* between phyto- and zooplankton and was mentioned in passing when describing plankton distribution in Chapter 6. One of the explanations of this relationship is that the zooplankton graze on the phytoplankton thus reducing their numbers, whilst the numbers of zooplankton increase. This is called the *grazing hypothesis,* which at present seems to be the most satisfactory explanation for the inverse phyto-zooplankton relationship.

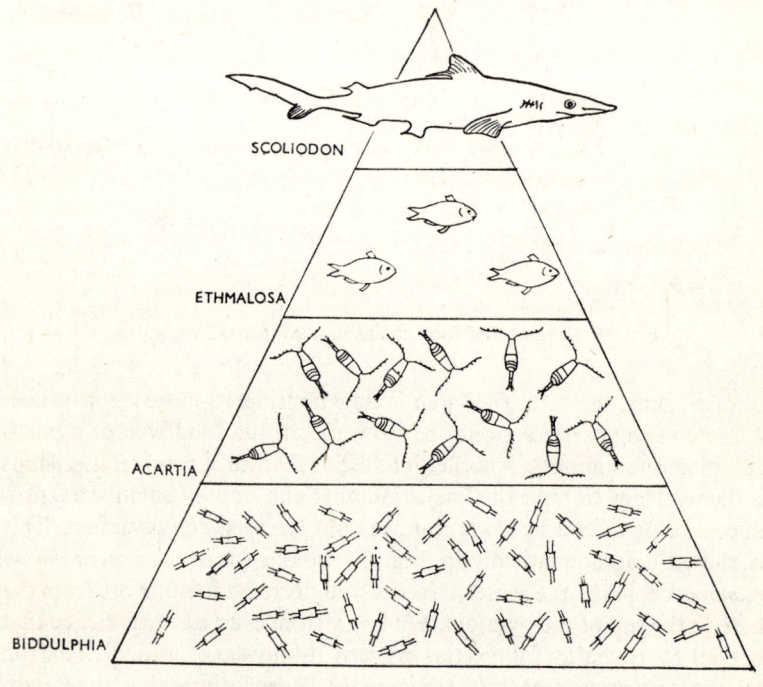

Fig. 77. Pyramid of numbers in non-parasitic animals (after Buchsbaum).

Other relationships

Broadly speaking, the relationship between any two species in a community may be *neutral, negative,* or *positive.* When they have no effect on one another, which is rare, the relationship is one of *neutralism.* When one or both organisms are adversely affected or inhibited, it is a negative relationship, and the food relationships already described are examples of what may be regarded as negative relationships. Another example is *parasitism.* When one or both organisms benefit and none is

THE INTERRELATIONSHIPS OF ANIMALS 159

at a disadvantage, we have a positive relationship, and **symbiosis** and **commensalism** are two common types.

A relationship between two animals in which tye loosely (i.e. not intimately) depend on each other without any adverse effects is called **commensalism**. Literally, it means 'at table together'—one animal consuming the unused food of another. The partners may, in fact, be capable of living by themselves, so the association is not obligatory. This type of relationship is common between sessile organisms and others which are motile, as exhibited by the relationship between sea anemones and hermit crabs. The sea anemone, because of its stinging cells, protects the crab, and in 'payment' for this the anemone has free transport and can also obtain particles of food, which are bound to reach it whenever the crab has a meal. There are several such associations especially in the sea between worms and sponges, worms and hermit crabs and so on. In several cases it has been shown that there is clear advantage without any danger to either party.

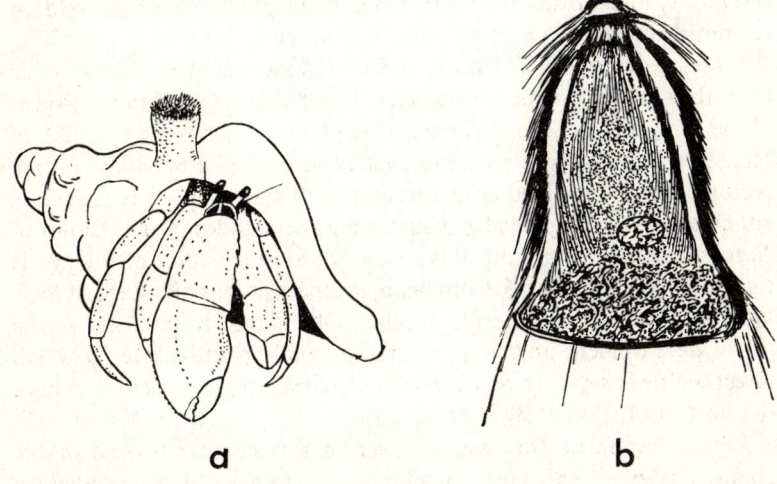

Fig. 78.
(*a*) Commensalism in hermit crab and sea anemone.
(*b*) Symbiotic flagellate of termites, *Trichonympha sp*.

Another type of association, similar to commensalism, is **symbiosis**. The difference between the two is that in symbiosis the association is more intimate, and is usually obligatory—that is, both animals cannot survive without associating. Although symbiosis may occur between two animals, more often it is between an animal and a plant. A well-known example of the latter type between a turbellarian and an alga is found in *Convoluta roscoffensis* in which an alga is associated, giving it a green colour. From the early stages of development, the cells of the animal are infected with this alga and without the alga the animal will not grow. Association between two animals of a symbiotic nature is found among the termites which require a population of certain flagellates *Trichonympha* in their alimentary canal in order to be able to digest woody substances. It has been found possible experimentally to cleanse certain termites of these flagellates with the result that they eventually die of starvation.

Finally, we come to *parasitism,* an intimate association of two animals or plants in which only one derives benefit to the detriment of the other. In many respects this is very like predation, except that the parasite, unlike a predator, does not set out (so to say) to kill the host for food in the way a predator kills its prey. In fact killing the host is a disadvantage to the parasite itself, because it is in its own interest that its host should remain alive! Generally, parasites exhibit a clear *host specificity,* and in this they also differ from predators which seldom restrict themselves to a single particular species.

When parasites, such as lice and fleas, live outside the bodies of their host, they are known as *ectoparasites.* When they live within the tissues of the host, they are *endoparasites.* These two categories are not sharply separable; for example, parasites which live in the oesophagus and the rectum, which are lined with ectodermal tissue, may be regarded as either ecto- or endoparasites. Ciliates and nematodes in the rectum of *Bufo*, for instance, fall into this category. Another point of interest is that some animals change from being ectoparasites at one stage of their life history to endoparasites in another. Others may be parasitic during larval development and non-parasitic as adults; the *warble fly* which infects cattle is a case in point. The larvae develop just under the skin of the host but the adult fly is non-parasitic.

Passing reference was made earlier in this chapter to one of the characteristics of parasites, namely, their extremely high reproductive rate. A second characteristic is that their food chains show an *inverted pyramid of numbers* opposite to the normal pyramid of numbers described for free-living animals. Instead of decrease in numbers and increase in size as the food chain lengthens, there is increase in numbers and decrease in size. As an example, if we start with a single host, say a dog, it may harbour hundreds of lice, and each louse, in turn, may harbour thousands of parasitic protozoa in its body.

Other parasitic characteristics include the development of attachment structures (such as *suckers, jaws,* and *hooks*); the *degeneration of diges-*

tive and locomotory structures; the development of **haemaphroditism and self-fertilization;** and a general ability to modify their life so that it fits intimately with that of the host. The study of parasites has become a subject in itself—parasitology—which is growing rapidly. It should be remembered, however, that to an ecologist it is just a study of one of the many relationships between animals.

I would like to end this section on parasites by mentioning a rather unusual relationship which does not quite fall within the usual definition of parasitism. Some abyssal fishes are known to develop a so-called **parasitic male** which remains small throughout life and is permanently attached to the female. In view of the great hazards of abyssal life, and the very low density of its fauna, animals seeking a mate would find it more difficult if they waited till maturity like other animals before attempting to do so. A fish which is able to select a partner very early in life stands a better chance, because at that stage there will be more individuals. The male, after attaching to the female, becomes fused with it, and due to certain hormone influences does not develop any further in size. Only the gonads develop, enabling it to fertilize the eggs of the female at the appropriate time. In this relationship, both parties derive benefit, indicating symbiosis, but the male is at a disadvantage in that it is prevented from normal growth. Also there is a difference from true symbiosis because we are dealing with two individuals belonging to the same species—an intraspecific relationship—whereas true symbiosis is interspecific. All that can be said, therefore, is that this is an example of **permanent association** which shows parasitic and symbiotic characteristics. The relationship is not as unique as it sounds because *Schistosoma*, a parasitic flatworm in the bladder of man, and *Syngamus trachea*, which infects trachea of poultry, also show a similar relationship between male and female. In both cases the male is greatly reduced in size.

Human ecology

One of the latest fields of ecological study is that of human ecology, and, broadly speaking, basic ecological concepts will apply to man as a species, *Homo sapiens*. However, we know that, unlike other animals, man has developed various means of controlling or modifying his environment; and more important still, the development of a 'culture' and other human values are important factors to reckon with.

One important aspect of human ecology is the study of human population. It is generally accepted that the growth of human populations should go hand in hand with the development of greater efficiency in food production. Going back to Malthus, whose *Essay on the Principles of Populations* is much quoted, we learn that populations have an inherent ability for exponential growth, tending to outstrip food supply. This does not necessarily occur in practice but there is no doubt that it is quite possible, as shown in Fig. 79. It is therefore necessary to try to increase the productivity of the biosphere adequately.

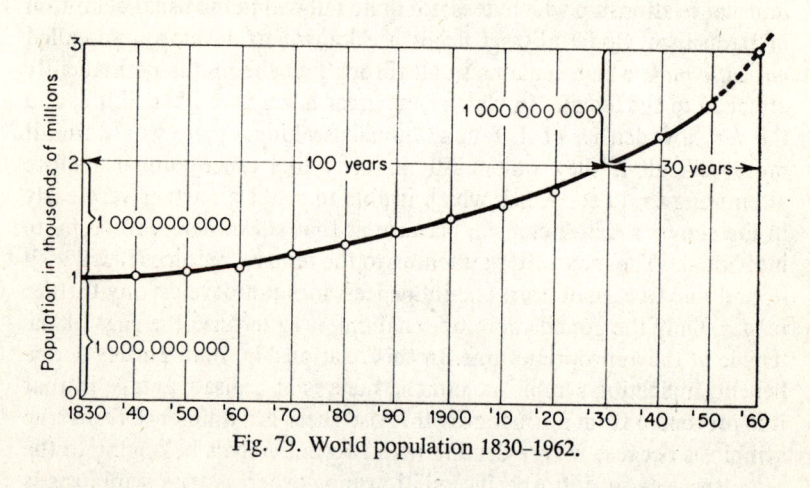

Fig. 79. World population 1830–1962.

Opinions differ somewhat on the subject of whether the world is in danger of overpopulation or not. Both optimistic and pessimistic views are held. However, there is no doubt that sooner or later some form of stabilization and control in human population will be essential when all the available sources of food on land and in the sea have been developed and tapped. There are methods of control which are not pleasant to consider; namely, modern warfare, pestilence, and other natural and man-made catastrophes which have been effective in the past. Today it is generally agreed that only *planned* methods will be effective in the long run.

Artificial methods of population control, in the form of contraceptive devices, are now used, and when these begin to operate satisfactorily, especially in parts of the world such as Asia, where the consequences of over-population are already manifest, a good start will have been made in tackling one of the world's most serious problems.

It is imperative that more and more efficient methods of producing food should be sought, so that the future of mankind may become more assured than it is at present.

Things to do

Work out the 'food-web' for some selected organisms in your area. Select the organisms bearing in mind the 'pyramid of numbers'. By examining the stomach contents of a given animal soon after it is caught, you can get an idea of its major food items.

Select Bibliography

BANNERMAN, D. A.
The Birds of West and Equatorial Africa. 2 Vols. Oliver and Boyd. 1953.
BARNES, H.
Oceanography and Marine Biology: A Book of Techniques. Allen & Unwin. 1959.
BOULENGER, G. A.
Catalogue of the Freshwater fishes of Africa in British Museum (N.H.). 4 Vols. Taylor and Francis. 1909–16.
BOOTH, A. H.
Small Mammals of West Africa. Longmans. 1960.
CANSDALE, G. S.
West African Snakes. Longmans. 1961.
ELGOOD, J. H.
Birds of West African Town and Garden. Longmans. 1960.
FOWLER, H. W.
The Marine fishes of West Africa. 2 Vols. 1936.
Bull. Am. Mus. Nat. Hist., **70**, pp. 1–1493.
HARDY, A. C.
The Open Sea, Vol. 1: *The World of Plankton.* Collins. 1956.
HARVEY, H. W.
The Chemistry and Fertility of Sea Water. O.U.P. 1955.
HOPKINS, B.
Forest and Savanna Heinemann. 2nd Edition 1974.
KEAY, R. W. J.
Vegetation Map of Africa. O.U.P. 1959.
MOORE, H. B.
Marine Ecology. Wiley. 1958.
NICOL, J. A. C.
The Biology of Marine Animals. Pitman. 1960.
The Nigerian Field.
A Journal published by the Nigerian Field Society. Vol. 1 1931 to present Vol. XXXVII (1972).
WADSWORTH, R. M. ed.
The measurement of the Environmental factors in terrestrial ecology. 8th Symposium of the British Ecological Society. Blackwell. 1968.
WICKSTEAD, J. H.
An introduction to the study of tropical plankton. Hutchinson. 1965.

Index

ABYSSAL FAUNA, 76, 95–8
— zone, *8*, 9, 14, 23
Accra, 65, 87
acid combining capacity, 30
adaptation for arboreal life, 127–9
— for behaviour, 49–50, 137
— for desert life, 144–5
— for intertidal life, 60
— for rapids zone, 110–11
— for savanna life, 135–6
— of animals, 37–51
aggregation, 154
antennal gland, 44
aphotic zone, *10*, 12, 14, 80
arboreal amphibia, 130
— birds, 130–1
— mammals, 132–3
— reptiles, 130

BATHYAL FAUNA, 76
— zone, *8*, 9, 14
bathypelagic, *8*, 80
bathyscaphe, 65, 98
bathysphere, 65
benthon, 40
biosphere, 7
biota, 7
black layer, 14
bromo-thymol blue, 24
buffer, 24
burrowing amphibia, 124
— mammals, 124
— reptiles, 124
brackish water, 10, 27, 39, 45, 68

CAKE—BIOLOGICAL, 3, Fig. 1
Cameroun, 57, 124, 145
chemical warfare, 136
chlorinity, 14
cleidoic egg, 50
commensalism, 159, Fig. 78

community characteristics, 156–8
— definition, 151
competition, 155
Congo, 119
consumers, primary, 156
— secondary, 156
— tertiary, 156
continental drift, 117
cresol red, 24
Cross river, 132
currents, Benguela, 21, 28
— convection, 21, 28
— Guinea stream, 21
— osmotic, 44, Fig. 20
— respiratory, 39
— tide, 33
— water, 28

DAHOMEY GAP, 119, 135
density of water, 27
— of population, 151
— optimum, 151
depth gauge, 18, Plate I
desert zone, 12, 15
diatoms, 82, 83, 103
dinoflagellates, 82–3
disphotic zone, *8*, 9, 12, 14
dissolved ammonia, 30
— carbon dioxide, 30
— gases, 29–30
— hydrogen sulphide, 30
— salts, 24
diurnal rhythm, 93
dredge, 64, Fig. 29

ECHO SOUNDER, 100
Ecology: behavioural, 117–18, *107*, Plates V, VI, X(d)
— branches, 4
— definition, 3
— history, 4
— human, 161–2
ecological balance, 147, 152
— factors, 16–36
— zones, 8
Ecosystem, 4
Ejirin, 70, 71
epilimnion, 20, *21*
euphotic zone, *8*, 9, *10*, 14
euryhaline, 45, 92
exoskeleton, 46

FACTORS, BIOTIC, 34
— ecological, 16
— edaphic, 33
— limiting, 34
— topographic, 34
feeding, ciliary, 41
— detritus, 124
— filter, 60
fishing festival, 30
— methods, 93, Plate III
food chain definition, 156
— in freshwater, 156–7, *157*
— in marine, 156–7, *157*
food web, 157
forest arboreal fauna, 127–34, Figs 63, 64, 66, 67
— birds, 130–1, Fig. 65
— fringing, 119
— galley, 119
— ground fauna, 125, Figs 61, 62
— high, 119
— mangrove, 119
— soil, 120
— soil fauna, 120
— tropical, 12, 14
freshwater birds, 112–15, Fig. 53
— fauna, 101–15, Figs 46–52
frictional resistance, 87
frustules, 83

GHANA, 57, 65, 87, 99, 101, 119
gill, 39, Fig. 18
grab, 64, Fig. 29
gregariousness, 136, Plate X(d)

HABITAT, 7, Figs 2 and 3
hadal zone, 9, 14, 23
Haeckel, Ernst, 4, 5
heredity, 5
humidity definition and measurement, 34
— in desert, 144
hygrometer, 34
hypolimnion, 20, *21*, 29

IBADAN, 109
intertidal fauna, 58–62, Figs 25, 27
— zone, *8*, 9, 14, 32, 33, 37

KAINJI, 101
kidney, 44
Kuramo, 70, 75

LAGOON FAUNA, 68–76, Figs 32, 35, 45
Lagos, 66, 68, 70, 75, 87, 89, 92
larva chironomus, *104*, *105*
— echinopluteus, 84
— eristalis, 104, 105
— megalopa, 84
— nauplius, 84
— nereid, 84
— of Branchiostoma, 84
— pelagic, 43
— pluteus, 84
— spionid, 84
— zoea, 84
lentic water, 10, 12, 14, 28, 101
Liberia, 132
light factor, 22
— meter, 23
— organ, 96
limbs jointed, *47–8*
— littoral zone, *10*, 12, 14
— lotic water, 10, 12, 14, 28, 101
— lung, 47
— pentadactyl, 47–8

MARIANA TRENCH, 9
mesh size, 80
methyl orange, 30
montane zone, 12, 14, 116
— birds, Fig. 73
— fauna, 145–6

NATURE CONSERVATION, 145, 146
— management, 146
nekton, 40, 80, 93, 96–100, 104–10, Figs 43, 45
neritic zone, 93
nets cast, 93, Plate III
— plankton, 80, 81, Fig. 34
— seine, 93, 100
— trawl, 93, Fig. 42
Niger river, 101
Nigeria, 57, 70, 87, 101, 119, 132
nitrate, 27
nitrite, 27, Fig. 14

OCEANIC ZONE, 93
organnelle, 43
osmoregulation, 43
osmosis, 38
overturn, 21, 29

oxygen content, 24, 29, Fig. 9
— concentration, 105

PARASITISM, 158, 160
patchy distribution of plankton, 88, 154
— of animals, 154
periphyton, 103
phosphate, 26, Fig. 13
photic zone, 80
pH definition, 23
— measurement, 24
— meter, 24
plankters, 80
plankton, 27, 40, 41, 80–93, 103–5, 157
— lagoon, 88
— nanno, 80
— phyto, 80, 83
— zoo, 80, 83
pool zone, *10*, 12, 14, 101
population control, 162
— characteristics, 151
— definition, 151
— density, 151–2
— dispersion, 154
— growth, 155
— world, 162, Fig. 79
potassium chromate, 24
pre-adaptation, 37–8
pressure, 23
protective coloration, 41–2, 48–50, 117, Figs 19, 22
pyramid of numbers, 157–8, Fig. 77

RAINFALL, 16, 28, Figs 5, 6, 12
rain gauge, 18
rapids zone, 12, 14, 110
region, Ethiopean, 117
— zoogeographical, 116, Fig. 54
relationships, intraspecific, 151
— interspecific, 151
— inverse, 157
rheotaxis, 112

SALINITY, Figs 11, 12, 14, 31
— measurement, 24–6, 39
— tolerance, 69
savanna animals, 135–43, Figs 68, 69
— birds, 137–9
— mammals, 140–3, Figs 70, 71, 72
— tolerance, 69

savanna types, 135
— zone, 12, 14, 116, Figs. 4, 56
seasonal distribution, 90–1, Fig. 40
secchi disc, 28
Sierra Leone, 132
silver nitrate, 24
soil science, 15
— fauna, 120–24, Figs 57–60
Sokoto, 19, *20*
stenohaline, 45
submarine illuminator, 23
subtidal fauna, 64–8, Figs 28, 30
— zone, *92*, 14
supratidal zone, 8, 14
— fauna, 55–8, Figs 23, 24
symbiosis, 159, Fig. 78
symmetry, bilateral, 41
— radial, 41

TEMPERATURE, 18, 29, 46, 116, Figs 7, 8
termite swarming, 18, 23
territorial behaviour, 117–19, Fig. 55
thermocline, 20, 21, Figs 9, 10
thermometer, types, 22
thigmotaxis, 111
tide, 30–3
— ebb, 33, Fig. 17
— flood, 33, Fig. 17
— neap, 31, Fig. 16
— spring, 31, Fig. 15
transparency, 27
tube feet, 41, 60
Tullgren funnel, 148
turbidity 28

VERTICAL MIGRATION, 23, 40, 92, 103
viscosity, 27
Volta river, 101

YANKARI GAME RESERVE, 148

ZONATION, 57, 65, 69, 101, 124–5
Zooplankton—permanent, 83, Figs 37–8
— temporary, 83–4, Fig. 36